PAINTING WITH PASTELS

PAINTING WITH PASTELS

AUBREY PHILLIPS

B.T. Batsford Ltd, London

To my dear wife Doris, whose help and encouragement made this book possible.

First published 1993

© Aubrey Phillips 1993

Typeset by Servis Filmsetting Ltd, Manchester
and printed in Singapore

Published by
B.T. Batsford Ltd
4 Fitzhardinge Street
London W1H 0AH

British Library Cataloguing-in-Publication data. A catalogue record for this book is available from the British Library.

ISBN 0 7134 7122 0

Complementary to this book is a sixty-minute video, *Painting with Pastels*, in which Aubrey Phillips can be seen painting some of the types of subject illustrated in this book. The video is available from the following address: APV Films, 6 Alexandra Square, Chipping Norton, Oxon OX7 5HL (*Telephone:* 0608 641798).

Jacket illustrations
(*Front*) *Red waterlilies*. 46 × 36 cm (18 × 14 in)
(*Back*) *Welsh farm*. 28 × 38 cm (11 × 15 in)

Page 1
Worcestershire wood, May.
38 × 28 cm (15 × 11 in)

Pages 2–3
Marguerites. 28 × 38 cm (11 × 15 in)

CONTENTS

INTRODUCTION

People often ask me which is my favourite medium, to which I find it difficult to give an honest reply. My usual answer is that it is the medium I happen to be using at the time. If I were ever marooned on the proverbial desert island with the choice of only one medium, however, I know that it would have to be pastel.

I love the feeling of the stick held in my fingers, and being able to look up at my subject, choose another stick and make further marks of a given shape. It is a spontaneous action, with nothing to come between me and my pigment, my support and my subject, with the added advantage of requiring no brushes and no mixing.

Pastel is a natural next step for a student who is familiar with pencil, pen and other related media, and who is venturing into the use of coloured pigments. It is also the ideal medium when working from nature, as hardly any equipment is needed and it is quick to use, allowing freedom of movement.

Pastel is an old medium. The earliest examples of its use have been traced back to ancient cave-dwellers of perhaps three thousand years ago. They used white chalk and various earth colours – including ochres, umbers and charcoal from the charred wood of fires – to practise their art on the walls of their caves, creating our first picture galleries. The fact that many of these paintings are still visible is ample proof of the permanence of the pastel medium.

Pastels are available today in a much more sophisticated form. The same earth colours are still used, together with new pigments, and are prepared, tested and presented in a convenient way. The basic colours are mixed with varying amounts of pipe or China clay, together with a binder such as gum Tragacanth.

The name pastel possibly derives from the preparation of the pigment into some form of 'paste'. This would be allowed to dry, having first been moulded into a convenient form for use. In this book I refer to artist's 'soft' pastels. These should not be confused with oil pastels, which are more greasy in texture and an entirely different medium.

SELECTION OF PASTELS

There is a very wide choice of first-class pastels available today. There is little point in quoting here a specific range of colours by name, as there are so many of them, presented in different ways. Some are numbered according to the various tints, from light to dark, but this does vary. The best way to choose a range is to visit your local stockist and select from his or her trays of separate sticks.

If you buy a large box of pastels already made up, there will be quite a number of sticks which you will rarely use if you intend to concentrate on landscapes. These will be the very bright colours, which look temptingly attractive on display. Some special selections (chosen for painting landscapes, portraits, and so on) are available

in box form. These will provide you with a basic range, to which could be added colours of your own choice.

If you are accustomed to working in oil, watercolour or acrylic, where a limited palette (from which other colours are mixed) is best, you may find it rather difficult to make a wise selection from such a vast range of pastel colours. To make this easier, obtain a pastel chart from your art supplier, look at one of your paintings and try to match up the actual colours with those available in the chart. Remember that these

are already mixed, although you will also be able to mix further colours in a limited way, as I will explain in due course.

You will soon become aware that it is the quiet greys and greens in their varying tonal strengths that will be most needed, with a few bright pinks, ochres and blues for contrast. Some of the names of these colours will be familiar: French ultramarine, burnt umber and burnt sienna, yellow ochre, and so on. These are presented in a number of sticks, through the tonal scale. There are subtle mixtures, too, which have

Summer garden, Crathes Castle, Kincardineshire. 28 × 38 cm (11 × 15 in)

self-explanatory names such as green- and red-greys, purple-brown and so on.

You will find it helpful to create a colour chart by making a mark with each stick on a sheet of mid-grey pastel paper. Write against each mark its colour and the tint number or reference. The wrapping-paper on each pastel will give this information, but the paper will be removed when the stick is used, and so you need to keep a note of the references in order to make replacements. The chart will also help to assess your range of colour and will reveal the need for additions.

PASTEL PAPERS

Paper is the usual support for pastel work, and its texture and tone form a very important part of the technique. Many different types and colours of pastel paper are available, ranging from cheap sugar paper (once used, as the name implies, for wrapping sugar), to the better-quality Canson Ingres, Fabriano and others. Sugar paper is suitable for quick sketches and experimental work, but, as it lacks much texture, it will not hold the pastel as well as other papers, and its colour is fugitive.

Some types of pastel paper are more openly textured on one side than the other, and, according to my subject, I choose whichever side I think will be most helpful for a particular painting. It is a good idea to take a piece of pastel across a corner of each side of the paper before starting work, to establish which is best for the subject.

Watercolour paper can be used with pastels, but, as this is white, it provides no help if a tonal background is required. This problem can be overcome by washing a tone of watercolour, acrylic or ink over the paper, having first stretched it to prevent cockling of the surface. I like a Not surface, as I find that the hot-pressed variety is too smooth to hold the pastel, and that the rough type has too much 'tooth', making it difficult for the pastel to cover sufficiently.

The fine-grained sandpaper used by woodworkers for smoothing down surfaces is very sympathetic to pastel work. This holds the medium very well, and a greater quantity can be loaded on to it, resembling the oil-painting technique.

Lake Bala. Study in black Conté crayon. 25 × 21 cm (6 × 8½ in)

Bala 23.8.86.

1

TECHNIQUES

There are a number of misconceptions about pastel, one of which is that it is useful only for slight, rubbed-in, insipid work. This is, of course, found to be far from the truth upon investigation of the paintings of pastel artists past and present. Among these have been Degas, Holbein, Manet, Whistler, Vuillard and also Turner, who used pastel for some of his inspired studies from nature. His atmospheric sketches of Dolbadarn Castle, made in 1799 when he was a young man of twenty-four, come to mind. He made six of these, and they provided important material for his future interpretation in oils.

I can never understand how the term 'pastel shades', meaning soft, delicate colours, ever came into being, as the depth of tone of the medium can be equal to anything done in oils, while watercolour is a transparent medium in which heavy darks do not apply.

Pastel is a permanent medium, chiefly because it is basically pure pigment with only additives of clay and a binder (which are inert),

while oils are liable to darken and crack with the passage of time. Many of the pastel paintings created by past masters are as fresh today as ever: look at Degas's ballet studies, for instance.

It is interesting to study Turner's love of tinted backgrounds. He described these as his 'colour beginnings', in which he blended tints together, both in transparent washes of watercolour and, at times, using opaque body colour. It seems that these backgrounds stimulated Turner's creative imagination when he applied pastel, pencil or other media over them, allowing the prepared backgrounds to show through where necessary. This of course relates particularly to pastel, where, the medium being opaque, the background may be covered or left exposed as required, at the same time creating an overall tone and colour harmony.

I am myself in favour of experimenting with the various possibilities of pastel. I once immersed an unsuccessful pastel painting under water for a few minutes, allowing the paper to

become limp. I then placed it back on the drawing-board, using gum strip round the edges to stretch the paper in the usual way. When it had dried out I found that the immersion had created a general softening of the forms, and I made use of this in certain passages, while strengthening it in others. The picture was exhibited and found a purchaser, so trying new ideas can be worthwhile!

I do not use a fixative on my paintings, as this tends to darken the work and disturbs the 'bloom' on the surface. I did, however, carry out an experiment with one picture by spraying the initial application of pastel, to allow further work without disturbing this first covering, and continuing to apply pastel and spray alternately (a technique sometimes used by Degas). The result was a rather dark, almost impasto surface with dramatic tonal contrasts, but resembling an oil painting. I decided that there was little point in making a pastel resemble an oil, but I had learned something from the experiment.

DIFFERENT METHODS OF APPLYING PASTELS

For this first exercise I chose a dark-toned Ingres paper, and five pastels of different colours. Having removed the paper from each I applied pieces of pastel, in lengths of about half an inch and laid flat on the paper at the top of the page, pressing firmly with deliberate strokes and easing off the pressure as my hand moved down (**A**). You will notice how a positive colour results from a firm pressure, pushing the pigment into the grain of the paper and giving greater coverage, but that the

paper shows through progressively more when a lighter touch is used. With a mid-blue pastel used flat, I then drew across the first colours with a fairly light pressure and allowed those underneath to show through, thereby creating a certain colour mixture.

At **B**, I used one deliberate downward stroke as opposed to the sideways movement of those at the top of the page. At **C** and **D** only the edge of the stick made contact with the paper, providing a line effect which suggests movement. It is possible to produce quite fine lines in this way, by selecting freshly broken sticks or those that have been used

Different methods of applying pastels.

for different strokes and worn down to sharp facets.

At **E**, I used worn sticks along the whole of their length, producing a long edge. In this case, the stick was laid flat and drawn with an up-and-down movement while the entire length of the pastel was kept in contact with the paper.

The sticks of pastel themselves, and the arrows, were drawn in with black Conté crayon, which is harder than pastel and can be sharpened with a penknife to produce a point as needed. This is helpful in pastel work when more precise drawing is required as pastels are too soft to allow any sharpening, although, as I have said, I make use of the broken edges and points which develop naturally in use.

PREPARATION OF PAPER FOR PASTEL WORK

In this demonstration I stretched a sheet of Bockingford paper, of 140 lb (300 gsm) weight, on to a drawing-board. When it was dry, I washed over it a prepared mixture of French ultramarine and burnt sienna acrylic paint. I blended the colours in two white saucers (white enabled me to assess the true colour values). In the first, French ultramarine prevailed, while burnt sienna predominated in the second. These were rather liquid washes, which flowed freely down the paper surface, as the drawing-board was set at an angle of about 25°.

With a two-inch decorator's brush, and starting at the top of the board, I applied the wash from the first saucer across the paper with broad strokes, allowing the liquid to collect at the base of each stroke. About halfway down I began to lay on the mixture from the second saucer to cover the remainder of the paper. I soaked up the excess at the base with the big brush, and left the board in position until dry.

As the wash was being applied in this way the colours separated, causing granulation, which

Stage 1: prepared Bockingford paper, stretched and washed over with acrylic paint. 36 × 48 cm (14 × 19 in)

Stage 2: the completed demonstration, with pastels applied over the acrylic wash to create different textures. 36 × 48 cm (14 × 19 in)

produced an attractive textured effect. A wide range of colours can obviously be used for this method of paper preparation, both with flat or gradated washes. It is particularly helpful where pronounced texture is required in the subject matter.

When the paper was completely dry, I began to use the pastels, applying them chiefly on their sides with varied pressure. This technique is also shown in the previous demonstration on page 10 at **A**, which made full use of the paper showing through as the pressure was lifted, but covered the textured paper where pressure was used.

Next, I sketched in the shape of a bridge with a suggestion of trees to its left. You can see from this how the pronounced texture produced in this way may apply to both foliage and old stonework. Below the bridge I rubbed in the pastel with my fingers. This worked the pigment down into the surface grain of the paper in much the same way as when applied firmly, but rubbing gave a smoother look which indicated the surface of water. In this way one surface can enhance the other by contrast, although too much rubbing can have a detrimental effect and spoil that valuable quality of pastel: its texture.

At the bottom of the sketch I applied the pastels with their edges, as shown on page 10 at **E**. Compare the texture produced on this prepared paper with that of the earlier demonstration.

CHURCH AND WET STREET

I chose a deep-stone Ingres paper for this picture, which provided a middle tone. I first applied pale blue for the sky, with which I carefully shaped up the church tower and other buildings in a 'negative' way by working around them. I repeated this process in the street area, rubbing the colour in to suggest the wetness. I then drew in firmly with a piece of black compressed charcoal, using varied pressure and taking care not to cover too much of the paper, as this was to play an important part in the overall tonal relationship.

The next step was to add pale cadmium yellow for the lights in the windows, and to rub in their reflections in the wet street with the other tones. The two figures provided human interest and scale. A putty eraser drawn across the street suggested drier areas.

To the right of the sketch, at **A**, you can see the three tones that I used, applied with varied pressure and rubbed across the centre to produce a softer effect.

At **B** are examples of the firm lines produced with pastel pencils. These are harder than 'soft' pastels, and are helpful when rather firm drawing is needed. They can be used together with black Conté crayon, or combined with soft pastel.

Church and wet street. 33 × 48 cm (13 × 19 in)

CHURCH AND POOL WITH LIGHTS

I used a deep-stone Ingres paper for this sketch, which I selected for its middle tone. I carefully laid in the pale blue sky, working around the shapes of the church tower and buildings, and leaving them as silhouettes. Repeating the pale blue for the water area, and, again,

Church and pool with lights.
33 × 48 cm (13 × 19 in)

leaving the paper for the reflections, I added dark green-grey for the trees and their reflections, and firmed up the dark areas in the trees with compressed charcoal.

I completed the work with pale cadmium yellow for the lights in the buildings and their reflections, softening the water area by rubbing in. To the right of the sketch I have shown the three pastels and the black compressed charcoal that I used. I have taken a putty eraser across these to show how they can be softened or lifted off altogether.

TREE STUDY

Shown opposite are three stages of a tree study on stone-coloured Canson paper. This provided a choice of surface, being rough on one side and smooth on the other. I chose the former to help with the texture of the foliage, although this meant that I had to rub in hard to obtain the smooth reflections.

At **A** I laid in a dark olive green for the middle tone of the tree, and used the same pastel for its reflection in the water below.

I rubbed this in to give a smooth look (you can see how the same pastel produces a darker tone when rubbed in, compared with the non-rubbed area above). This dark tone in the water area was suitable for the reflection in the finished sketch, shown at C.

At B I added a lighter green, repeating this in the water and rubbing it in.

At C I firmly laid in a dark burnt umber over the two greens for the shadowed foliage and to suggest the trunk and branches, repeating these tones in the water area and rubbing in. I completed the study with a pale Prussian blue for the sky, which was also repeated in the water, and rubbed it in. Finally, I dragged the pastel lightly over the reflections – without rubbing – to suggest a breeze-ruffled surface.

BEACH STUDY: REFLECTIONS

To the right of the next sketch (see overleaf) are the three pastels with which I worked on fine-grained

Tree study. 24 × 34 cm (9½ × 13½ in)

sandpaper: light Prussian blue, mid-blue-grey and dark burnt umber. I have lifted out the pastel strokes in the centre with an eraser to show a softer effect.

Rubbing in firmly with pale Prussian blue for the sky, I echoed this in the wet beach below. This was followed with blue-grey for the distant headlands and their reflections in the sands. Next, I boldly blocked in the cliffs on the right and the balancing rocks to the left with dark burnt umber, and carried this into the beach area below. I used a sharp edge which had developed on the burnt umber pastel to draw in the two figures and their reflections.

All the time I took care not to cover the entire surface of the paper, as its mid-tone of warm colour played a significant part in the work. I completed the study by taking a handy piece of mounting card and using it to rub in the beach area of the foreground quite firmly. (I know from past experience not to rub in firmly with my finger as it is not pleasant to sandpaper one's skin off.) I used an eraser to take off some of the dark cliff reflections on the right.

I only needed to use three colours of pastel for this small study, but the tonal contrasts were important. If I had worked it up into a larger-scale picture, I would have needed several more colours, while being careful to keep within the colour and tonal relationships already established in the sketch. I find that it is often helpful to begin with a small study like this one before embarking on something more ambitious, and would certainly recommend this practice to anyone fresh to pastel work.

At the bottom right of the sketch I have shown some of the shapes of mounting card that I use, although any type of rigid card would be suitable. I cut out the shapes with a Stanley knife.

Beach study: reflections. 24 × 34 cm (9½ × 13½ in)

2

COMPOSITION

Composition is the basis upon which a picture is built, whatever medium it is in. No matter how clever we may be with our colour, tone or drawing, unless a picture has a sure foundation it is bound to fail. The composition is my first consideration when planning a picture. If I analyse my subject when I am first attracted to it, I realize that it is basically the composition which appeals: that is, the balance of the main features.

Nature does not provide ready-made subjects for us to copy; we need to compose them ourselves. Nature affords us the raw materials, which we need to distil, casting out the impurities, to produce the end result of fine art. To a very large extent, this is dependent on our own personal feelings and taste, and, of course, experience. In this context it is interesting to study the subject matter that Turner used, and to compare it to the actual paintings he produced.

Whenever I contemplate a possible subject, I usually spend quite a time just looking and considering whether it is better suited to an upright or a horizontal format. I look for an object – such as a building, a group of interesting trees, a single tree, or even a section of the subject – where I can create a focal point by, perhaps, using a play of light. The use of a road or river to lead the eye towards that area can also be helpful, and you will see examples of this in many of the pictures in the book.

When planning a composition, it may be necessary to walk around and view the subject from different positions, perhaps making thumbnail sketches, before deciding how to proceed. This is time well spent and will often prevent the disappointment caused when, well advanced with a picture and pleased with our colour, tone and drawing, the sad realization begins to dawn that the composition is poor.

Simplification is very important. I select the elements that I need for my picture, and in doing so I may bring into my composition objects that are not within my subject area, and leave out others. It is often helpful to look at a subject with half-closed eyes, seeing it in blurred tones, or to look at it through a small piece of glass that has been treated by holding it in a candle flame long enough to become smoked.

In the four sketches shown overleaf (top), alternative compositions have been used. The example in **A** shows a symmetrical lake-and-mountain composition. This is unnatural – a rather extreme example of what is best avoided. The composition in **B** is a more satisfactory arrangement, with the distant mountain peak set to the left and the slopes of the other mountains placed lower down, avoiding the corners of the picture. The foreground leads into the composition instead of cutting straight across it.

In C, the large cliffs on the right of this coastal view make an unbalanced design, with the horizon line of the sea cutting through the centre, and the edge of the water running into the left-hand corner of the paper. At **D**, in

Alternative compositions.

contrast, the horizon and cliffs are set lower, as if viewed from further back and with more interesting shapes to them. I have brought in rocks to the left at the water's edge, to balance the headlands on the right, and have avoided the edge of the water leading to the corner. Clouds have been added, curving down and leading the eye towards the cliffs. This provides a contrast to the straight horizon of the sea and base of the cliffs.

The sketches shown below left give two more pairs of alternative compositions. In **A**, we have a composition with a church spire placed in the centre and equally massed trees on either side, which, with their reflections in the lake, make a formal pattern. In **B**, I set the water's edge lower down, avoiding the halfway position, and placed the church spire further back and a little to the left. I increased the size of the tree group on the right, bringing it forward, introducing more detail and deepening the tone, which, together with the reflections, makes a more natural composition.

In **C**, there is a formal arrangement, with the bridge set centrally and a large tree with a smaller one on each side. The reflections echo the formality, with the banks of the river on each side adding to the effect. In **D**, the large tree is placed to the left and nearer to the smaller one. The small tree on the right helps to give balance, and the reflections of trees and bridge create a less formal composition.

In the two charcoal studies below and overleaf we have a further development of the composition at **B** (opposite page, bottom), with the church spire and trees reflected in the water. As I have already mentioned, I find it interesting to explore the potential of a subject by the use of small studies depicting different viewpoints. Compare these two studies. In the first, with the horizontal format, I made use of the trees and other features on each side. In the second I found that the upright shape was helpful in expressing the height of the church spire and trees on the right.

PLACING OF MAIN INTEREST

A successful composition depends on a centre of interest, on which the eye can rest and focus once it has passed over the whole of the picture. In most of my pictures I find that the centre of interest is in the middle distance, often accentuated by a play of light and shade. In the studies of wildflowers and waterlilies on pages 21–3, I have diverged from this by focusing interest on the foreground in each case.

(Below and overleaf) Charcoal studies showing the development of a composition into different formats.

It is usually necessary to include more detail in a focal area than in other parts of a painting, but it is essential not to overdo this. We do, of course, actually *see* more detail in a foreground, but it is better to simplify this when dealing with a picture that has a focal point in the distance or middle distance. In these pictures, with the centre of interest in the foreground, I needed rather more detail, but only enough to carry conviction. The three pictures were painted on fine-grained sandpaper.

I chose an upright format for this study of *Wildflowers*. This helped me to look down into the nearer flowers, seeing them mostly full-faced but becoming more elliptical as they receded. Using dark olives and burnt umbers as a strong background to the light tones of the flowers, I gradually introduced darkish green-greys further away, with mid-blue-greys in the background. I applied more detail to the nearer areas, lessening this as I moved further back, and made use of warm colours as far as possible in the foreground, adding cooler tints as I receded.

Wildflowers. 43 × 30 cm (17 × 12 in)

For the composition of *Red waterlilies* (opposite), I again chose an upright shape. The design, based on the elongated forms of the reflections in the water, contrasted with the more horizontally drawn lilies and particularly with their elliptically-shaped leaves. The reeds also introduced a diagonal feeling. The dark reflections were important as seen against the light blooms and leaves, and it was essential that the latter were depicted lying flat on the surface of the water.

The horizontal design of *White waterlilies* was based on a lower eye level than the previous two flower studies. I was therefore able to include the far shore of the lake and some distant trees, although these were treated quite simply so

White waterlilies. 28 × 46 cm (11 × 18 in)

as not to detract in any way from the foreground interest. Scale played an important part in creating recession, with the large lily on the left contrasting with the others, which diminished in size as they receded into the distance.

Red waterlilies. 43 × 30 cm (17 × 12 in)

3

WORKING FROM NATURE

There could not possibly be a more convenient medium than pastel for working outdoors, as very little equipment is required. I take a piece of plywood or fibreboard measuring 41 × 28 cm (16 × 11 in) to which I secure a selection of pastel papers with bulldog clips. This includes fine-grained sandpaper and sugar paper, varying in tone and colour. Having about a dozen sheets of paper below the one selected for use provides a pad on which to work and prevents the feeling of the hard grain of the board beneath.

My method of preparing paper is to take a full-sized sheet, fold it in half and cut along the fold. I then fold each half sheet, and, without cutting these, work on one quarter sheet only, leaving the other quarter to fold over my sketch to protect it.

I carry my pastels (with the papers removed) in a handmade wooden box, divided into compartments to segregate the colours. This has a tightly-fitting padded lid and a carrying handle.

I put cooking flour in with the pastels, in which they can move around in transit and be kept clean, but this needs to be changed from time to time as it becomes discoloured. The lid acts as a seal, preventing the flour from escaping when the box is carried.

I also take on painting trips a sketchpad of cartridge paper measuring 30 × 43 cm (12 × 17 in) for black-and-white work, a few sticks of charcoal and Conté, a kneadable putty eraser and pencils varying from 2B to 6B. I also have two felt-tipped pens, one with a fairly broad tip, and the other a fine tip, and I usually carry a 'biro' pen in my pocket, which I find useful at times. Lastly, for hand-cleaning after using pastel or charcoal I take a damp cloth in a plastic bag. All these items are stowed in a pack which can be slung over my shoulder, allowing me to walk around freely in search of subjects.

I usually sit on a folding stool with my board on my knees and the pastels placed on a plastic sheet on the ground where I can easily

reach them; this prevents them becoming lost or ruined by moisture. I once spoiled a selection by placing a cardboard box on a beach that was more damp than I realized, with the result that the moisture seeped up from below into the pastels. Another safeguard is a second sheet of plastic, which can be placed quickly over the pastels and sketch in case of a sudden rainstorm.

I do not normally use an easel for outdoor work, although there are times when a composition is better viewed from a standing position. If this is the case, I would use an easel, placing the pastels on the stool to bring them within reach. Standing or sitting, you will need to move back from your work from time to time to get an overall impression of its progress.

On a persistently rainy day in Pembrokeshire, I was sitting in the car hoping that the weather would improve enough to allow me to get out and do some pastel work on the beach. Not liking to waste time or opportunity when I recognized a possible subject in front of me, however, and being well prepared for such a situation with some sheets of sugar paper clipped to my board, I took a biro from my pocket, switched on the windscreen wipers and set to work. The resulting sketch is shown below.

I freely attempted to capture the main elements of the composition, making a few written notes of colours and effects, which would be helpful if I decided to work up a picture from the sketch in the studio later. The inclusion of the figures was helpful in giving scale.

I then carried out another study (shown beneath the first sketch) in the same way, but from a slightly different position.

Biro sketches on sugar paper made from inside the car in the rain.

Pastel study of *Llyn Nantle, north Wales.* 23 × 38 cm (9 × 15 in)

Additional reference sketch of *Llyn Nantle.*

The next example, shown below, was a 'back-up' sketch. I had already made a pastel study of this subject – *Llyn Nantle, north Wales* (above) – but as there were some very impressive shapes in the mountain contours which attracted me, I felt the need for more precise information. I quickly drew this in with a fine-pointed fibre-tipped pen on sugar paper. The beautiful picture of the same scene, produced by the great Welsh painter, Richard Wilson, came to my mind.

On another occasion, the sun was setting low on the horizon after a fine summer day, and, having been concentrating on working along the estuary, I took a quiet walk to relax. I didn't have to go far before I saw an attractive group of boats silhouetted against the light – simple, but impressive in shape. I just couldn't let this go without doing something about it, so with my sketchbook of cartridge paper I quickly drew in the essentials with a broad fibre-tipped pen (opposite page, top).

I felt that the composition looked promising at this stage, but was aware that, if I were to make any more of it, there would have to be some balancing form on the right. Looking around, I found there were more boats further away with sheds behind them, although they were too far to the right to come within my field of vision. To solve this problem I simply moved my position slightly and brought them in a bit closer.

I worked quickly, concentrating chiefly on composition and tone, and still using the broad fibre-tipped pen. This dried almost straight away, so I swiftly covered large areas of the drawing with a length of soft charcoal, using it flat on the surface. This gave the tone of the clouds, and of the boat shadows that were cast across the foreground by the low sun. I also added some solid darks to the boats and sheds.

Next I took a putty eraser and, pressing in firmly, established the light sky behind the boats and the light across the beach. A great advantage was that I could do this without sacrificing the fibre-pen drawing of the boats.

This was the kind of subject that one can see in an instant, in which the conditions at that moment are the main feature. Had I made myself more comfortable and spent considerable time working on the sketch, the light would have changed and the subject disappeared. I had probably seen the boats earlier in the day, but they had not caught my attention then.

This type of sketch can be worked from and translated into colour in the studio, although it would still be the tonal contrasts and simple shapes that were the most important features. On reflection, I thought that a warm glow in the sky would add interest.

Preliminary composition sketch of boats in fibre-tipped pen.

The completed sketch in fibre-tipped pen and charcoal.

I painted this picture, *Early spring on the Wye*, on one of those lovely mornings towards the end of winter which sometimes surprise and delight us, making us realize that spring is almost upon us again. This scene is a stretch of that loveliest of rivers, the Wye, where it flows through Herefordshire on its way to join its larger sister, the Severn.

I chose a fairly high viewpoint from which to work. This presented the prospect of an attractive curve of the river, merging into the soft light which veiled the forms of the distant hills and was reflected in the water.

The dark tones of the near trees on the right contrasted splendidly against this, and were balanced by the more distant trees, together with their reflections, across the river on the left. Their warm colours were reflected, too, enhanced by the soft light which brightened the bank on the right and cast shadows from the nearer trees across the grass.

I used fine-grained sandpaper for this picture, working in the soft sky, the distance and the water, but using more texture in the foreground to the right. On the whole, this was a natural composition which needed to be treated as simply as possible. My main objective was to convey light, distance and atmosphere.

Early spring on the Wye. 28 × 36 cm (11 × 14 in)

As I have already mentioned, one of the many attractions that pastel holds for me is its spontaneity. On a certain calm winter day, I was invited by friends to take a trip along the River Avon in their canal longboat, which had been converted for use as a holiday home. I felt that this could really be a fine chance to make use of the immediacy of pastels, and was pleased to accept the opportunity of producing a few sketches from the middle of the river, instead of the usual views from its banks. Two of the sketches that I made are shown opposite.

I positioned myself in the bows, with my pastels on the deck at my side and my drawing-board firmly placed on some superstructure. I chose some sheets of mid-grey Ingres paper, which I felt would be appropriate for the soft, light, misty effect of the day. Travelling at about walking pace, the journey took us through part of the Vale of Evesham.

As the river wound about in some sections I found it difficult to view sufficiently far ahead to establish a composition. As soon as I saw a fairly straight stretch coming up, however, I quickly set to work, first of all setting the eye level which I would have to maintain. I soon discovered that I had to deal quickly with any large foreground trees, setting them down to scale before we had passed them. As they were chiefly willows I was usually able, as they came near, to find in one what I had missed in another. I had more time to study distant shapes, which were for the most part soft and grey, but as they came closer they naturally became clearer, and I had to remember to keep their soft, distant tones. As it was a rather grey day I did not need to bring many pastels into use – just half-a-dozen or so – which helped in my speed of working.

Sketching under such conditions certainly made me look quickly at the subject as I set it down, dealing only with the essentials. It was a good exercise in breadth of treatment. The sketches shown are just as I produced them, and were intended for use as a basis for further work – not only in pastel, but perhaps also in oils or watercolour. I have, in fact, made use of them on several occasions. I mostly used the pastels on their sides, laying in certain passages quickly, and making use of the edges where more clearly defined lines were required.

On the Avon. Two sketches carried out from the bow of a boat, each 25 × 32 cm (10½ × 12½ in)

4

THE PAINTER'S EYE

Casting our minds back to the dawn of history, we find that artists have played a very large part in shaping and influencing the lives of their fellow creatures, creating what we now refer to as 'Civilization'. We can marvel today at the work of artists and craftsmen of ancient Egypt and Greece, and later of Florence, Venice and Rome, reaching a peak in those Italian cities during the flowering of the Renaissance.

An instance that comes to mind is the way in which the classical painters of the seventeenth century influenced the creation of many of Britain's country estates. It was the work of two French painters, Claude and Poussin – especially their pictures of Italian scenery – which caused the landowners to have their parklands laid out in a similar manner. This usually included an example of what we now term a 'folly', strategically placed and looking very much like some of the classical temples portrayed in their pictures. This transformation of the landscape was usually placed under the direction of that well-known expert, 'Capability' Brown.

It is difficult for us to realize today, when landscape subjects feature so widely in paintings, that until the seventeenth century when Claude and Poussin made them acceptable, they were not generally considered suitable material. Until other painters in the eighteenth century followed their lead, landscapes – particularly of mountain scenes – were avoided as barren wildernesses.

Thankfully, we feel very differently today, and we owe this to artists and poets of the past, who have opened our eyes and enabled us to see beauty in unexpected places. It was John Constable who said: 'I never saw an ugly thing in my life, for let the form of an object be what it may, light, shade and perspective will always make it beautiful.' He showed this endlessly in his work, and, together with his illustrious contemporary Turner, added greatly to the enrichment of the human race. I have been reminded many times of Constable's significant words, for instance when I have seen an industrial landscape (which under normal circumstances would, I agree, be a blot on the landscape) transformed by the play of light through steam and smoke into a scene of beauty.

Using sugar paper, I made the quick study of *Industrial landscape, south Wales* (opposite, top) on the spot, attempting to convey an impression of the scene, with the dramatic light in the sky dominating the subject. I was not interested in the industrial buildings as such, but in their tones and basic shapes, which provided the setting for the main theme: the play of light.

I painted *Industrial landscape, south Wales, evening* (opposite) on fine-grained sandpaper. I rubbed in the soft, light areas of the sky, followed by the darker clouds and more distant, vague shapes of the chimney stacks and buildings, and gradually worked forward with

Industrial landscape, south Wales, evening. 26 × 36 cm (10 × 14 in)

darker greys towards the warmer buildings in the foreground. I laid these in more firmly, and used a black Conté stick to define their shapes clearly against the softer background. The warm colour of the paper, together with its texture, helped to bring this area forward. The light from the sky, reflected in the water, contrasted with the darker buildings and added to this effect.

(Right)
Industrial landscape,
south Wales. 20 × 31 cm (8 × 12 in)

A wet night. 23 × 33 cm (9 × 13 in)

I have no doubt that most people would class the kind of scene shown in *A wet night* (above) as unpleasant, to say the least. I have on many occasions had to drive home through the outskirts of Birmingham under such conditions and been fascinated by the play of light reflected in the wet streets. I used a dark brown paper for this rather low-key subject.

When I was driving over the Cotswolds on a cold and dull winter's day – not on the whole a very pleasant experience – I came across the subject in *A foggy day in the Cotswolds* (opposite). I was attracted to the way in which the fog simplified everything into vague, mysterious shapes, seeming to increase the scale of otherwise insignificant objects so that they took on dignified forms. Ash and oak trees by the roadside reared stark, bare branches skyward like ivy-mantled giants, standing out in contrast to the soft tones of the distant, fading trees and hedgerows.

On returning home I made a quick impression on cartridge paper of the effects I had seen. I used a broad fibre-tipped pen for the nearer trees, and laid over it tones of charcoal, holding the stick on its side to make wide sweeps. I then lifted out areas with a putty eraser to denote the light; this was used quite boldly as I knew it would only remove the charcoal and leave the pen drawing intact. The man walking with his dog added a sense of scale.

A foggy day in the Cotswolds.
33 × 28 cm (13 × 11 in)

DEMONSTRATION: GALE ON THE SUTHERLAND COAST

The coast of Sutherland in north-west Scotland is wild, remote and open to the full fury of Atlantic gales. Sandy beaches with great scattered rocks lie below towering cliffs that have been sculpted by the forces of nature over countless ages. These form the home of many seabirds, which add their cries to the tumult of the pounding seas.

I found myself urgently considering how to respond to such conditions. Any attempt to convey a convincing interpretation in terms of paint seemed a very daunting prospect, to say the least. I found what protection I could from the wind and spray by sheltering in the lee of a large rock, and tried to analyse what was happening.

A strong wind was blowing off the sea and bringing large waves racing in towards the cliffs, against which they were flung before shattering into columns of spray and dispersing in a few seconds. At the moment of impact against the rocks, the waves appeared white in places but a translucent blue-green in others. They tended to break at fairly regular intervals and form into more or less the same shapes. There was, of course, a sound reason for this, as the wind continued to blow from the same direction, driving the water on to fissured rocks, which channelled the water along in chiefly the same way each time.

Under such conditions it was quite apparent how nature had created such sculpted forms on the face of the cliffs. Realizing that I was fortunate in being able to observe this from firm (if not dry) land, I was reminded of Turner's experience when he set out from Harwich aboard the *Ariel* on a wild night and was soon involved in a violent storm. Never one to lose an opportunity for capturing a subject, he had himself lashed to the mast of the ship for four hours in order to observe the might of the storm, although with some doubts of surviving it. His

---

Three charcoal sketches of *Gale on the Sutherland coast*, the last of which was used as the basis for the finished painting.

interpretation of this first-hand experience remains for us to see today, in his oil painting of 1842, *Snowstorm, steamboat off a harbour's mouth, etc.*

Bringing myself back to my own situation, it was important to try to understand what I was attempting to convey in this painting. I made a few tentative impressions, but, at the same time, realized that anything I could do would be pretty feeble compared to the forces of nature. The three charcoal studies shown here are memory impressions made soon after returning to base. I used charcoal on cartridge paper for these, with fibre-tipped pen and compressed charcoal to sharpen up parts of the second sketch.

STAGE 1

In the first stage of this painting I used an underpainting of acrylic combined with black Indian ink. I had a sheet of 300 gsm (140 lb) Bockingford watercolour paper stretched on a drawing board, set on the table in the studio at an angle of about 25°.

I treated the paper first of all with a wash of liquid acrylic paint, as described on pages 11–12, using a mixture of French ultramarine and burnt sienna applied with a three-inch Hake brush on dry paper. I did not cover the entire surface of the white paper with the wash, but left an area where I wanted to convey the foam of the breaking waves. This white paper expressed luminosity better than white pastel would have done.

As I applied the wash I took care to soften the edges surrounding the white area with a sponge, before the wash dried out. I also lifted off an area below this (which had been covered by the wash) to suggest a reflection which would occur in the sands. I had no

Stage 1 of Gale on the Sutherland coast. 36 × 50 cm (14 × 20 in)

intention of laying a perfectly flat wash as it would be mostly covered with the pastel later, but I needed to lay it on quickly before it dried out leaving hard edges.

STAGE 2

Before the acrylic wash had dried, I began to apply Indian ink. This gave some really strong darks, which blended together to produce soft edges. I prepared the ink in two white saucers so that I could take it up with the brushes. One saucer contained ink straight from the bottle; the other held ink diluted with water according to the tones required.

I then washed in a darker tone in the sky to the left with burnt sienna, and shaped up the distant headlands with a mixture of burnt sienna and French ultramarine (with the latter predominating), which blended into the still-moist sky.

Next, I introduced the ink for the strong, dark rocks on each side of the foam area and on the left of the picture, diluting it for the softer edges and for the wet sands below with their reflections. While these washes were still wet, I added burnt sienna for the nearer areas of rocks, this warm colour contrasting with the cooler French ultramarine mixture behind. I was careful throughout to keep the white passages of paper clear of the washes.

THE FINISHED PAINTING
(See overleaf)

The final stage was to apply the pastel over the now-dry under-painting. This gave me a strong background to work over and, of course, I wanted to make use of it

---

Stage 2 of *Gale on the Sutherland coast*. 36 × 50 cm (14 × 20 in)

The finished painting of *Gale on the Sutherland coast*. 36 × 50 cm (14 × 20 in)

in the final work. As some very hard edges had developed, however, I needed to deal with them by rubbing in with the pastel.

Beginning with the sky, I indicated the storm clouds, which were sweeping in and softening the distant headlands, with the use of a soft, warmish grey. I also used this colour over the foreground beach area, and rubbed into it some of the reflected colour of the

rocks and foam. Over these soft passages I dragged a dark tone of burnt umber, without rubbing, which suggested the texture of pebbles and seaweed flung up by the waves, in contrast to the smooth, rubbed-in effect of the wet sands. The rough surface of the paper helped here.

For the sea in the centre of the work and for parts of the breaking waves, I dragged light green-grey together with pale blue across the surface of the paper, which helped in portraying the shattered water and flying-foam effect. I made use

of the sharp edges of the rocks, which had been washed in with the ink, to enhance this effect by contrast.

The gulls wheeling round, together with the figures, gave a feeling of life and scale to the scene, and the bright clothing worn by the two people helped to give an accent of colour to what was mostly a low-key subject. Tone played a vital part in this picture, and the dark of the rocks provided a necessary contrast in giving value to the light foam of the breaking waves.

5

WATER

Water plays an important part in my paintings of the landscape. Nature is often seen at its most dramatic at the dividing point between sea and land, or where a scene is reflected in the tranquil water of a lake or pool. As it is so quick and easy to work with, pastel is the ideal medium for painting water.

FALLING WATER

I experienced Niagara Falls on a day towards the end of winter, when melting snows were increasing the volume of water of the Falls. I say that I 'experienced' Niagara, for I feel that is a truer description than just 'seeing' it. It is easy to understand why the Iroquois Indians named it 'Thunder of Waters'. One experiences the great roar of cascading water and feels at times the drifting spray rising from a great boiling cauldron, into which ice floes slide at intervals to be churned around the great abyss.

If ever there was a time when I have felt insignificant before the forces of nature, this was it. How on earth was I to respond to it all, knowing that *something* should be done – if only an attempt to get an impression in charcoal on white cartridge paper?

In my charcoal study of *Niagara* (overleaf) I made use of the dark tones of the trees in the foreground, which contrasted well with the light foam. A little rubbing-in and lifting off with a putty eraser helped to convey the light spray and clouds of mist rising from below.

On returning to base, I translated the charcoal sketch into pastel for the finished painting of *Niagara* (see page 43). I worked on a piece of deep-stone Ingres paper, first establishing the areas of falling water by dragging pieces of light blue-grey and green-grey pastel on their sides. I allowed the paper to show through in parts for the upper areas of the Falls, and blended the tones together lower down to create a misty effect.

I then worked around the tree shapes and foreground rocks, leaving the natural tint of the paper to give me a basic tone.

Into this I put dark burnt umber and deep olive green, still leaving the paper uncovered in places, which helped to convey a unified dark tone. Mid-tints of blue-grey provided the distance above the Falls against a soft sky of pale cobalt blue and blue-greys blended together. Next, I firmly drew in the trunks and branches of the foreground trees, and the rocks, and added some white pastel for the lighter, falling water.

The technique of using the pastels with varied pressure was important here in dealing with the falling water. A firm application of the white pastel produced a much more positive light – indicating the foam – than when applied with less pressure, allowing the dark paper to show through to a greater degree. The same technique obviously applied when using the other light colours in the area of falling water to create a contrast with the rubbed-in areas of mist.

Charcoal study of *Niagara*.

(Opposite)
Niagara. 35 × 25 cm (14 × 10 in)

DEMONSTRATION: FALLS AT GLENCOE

It is difficult to associate the Pass of Glencoe with anything other than the grim history of clan warfare, particularly that terrible night in February 1692 when the Campbells massacred their hosts, the MacDonalds. I have seen the glen through blinding snow when it was easy to imagine that foul deed, but I have also travelled along it in warm spring sunshine with primroses sprinkling the slopes in bright array. On one occasion I spent a night there sleeping (or trying to sleep) in the car, and it was an unforgettable experience, just before dawn, to see the Northern Lights playing behind the great sombre peaks.

I have found many painting subjects along this renowned glen.

I carried out the charcoal sketch below after rain, when the river flowed swiftly down its rocky bed. Charcoal helped to capture the essential character of the scene, and gave me a chance to work out the composition and the strong contrasts of light and shade.

(See opposite for the four stages of painting)

STAGE 1

Although my charcoal study was horizontal in format, I decided on an upright composition for the painting itself, in order to give greater depth to the falls. I chose a grey Canson paper and, with a mid-grey pastel, drew in the main shapes of the valley.

STAGE 2

The next step was to block in the sky with light French ultramarine, and to darken the lower slopes of the valley with a dark purple-grey.

STAGE 3

At this point I darkened the near left-hand slopes of the valley further with purple-grey, and the right-hand slopes and the rocks in the falls with dark burnt umber. I used French ultramarine in the sky, and drew this lightly across the area of the falls.

STAGE 4

Next, I strengthened the darks of the right-hand slopes and the rocks to the left of the falls as well as those in the falls themselves. I added light and mid-tints of green-grey to the water area, and a touch of light red-grey for the rocks on each side of the river.

(Left)
Charcoal study of *Falls at Glencoe*.

(Opposite)
Stages 1 to 4 of *Falls at Glencoe*.
37 × 27 cm (14½ × 10½ in)

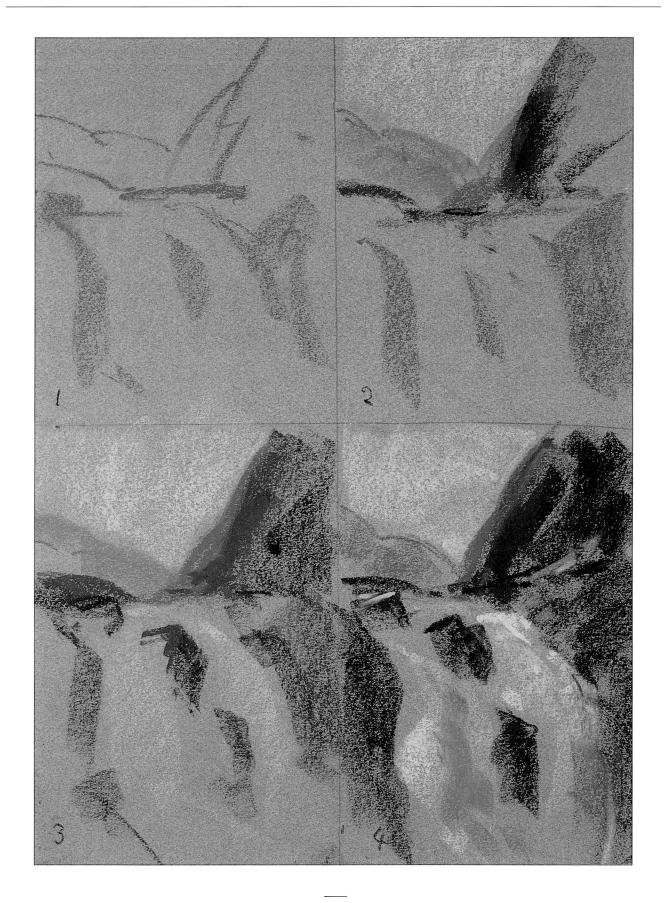

THE FINISHED PAINTING

I completed the work with the same pastels, building up the formation of the rocks and adding dark and mid-olive greens to those on the left in the foreground. I developed the patterns made by the falling water, adding a little cerulean blue and white for the

---

(Opposite)
The finished painting of *Falls at Glencoe.* 37 × 27 cm (14½ × 10½ in)

Falls at Abergynolwyn. 25 × 32 cm (10 × 12½ in)

highlights. Finally, I shaped up the forms of the near rocks with black Conté crayon.

I used a broad fibre-tipped pen to draw in the basic shapes of trees and rocks in *Falls at Abergynolwyn*, a study on light grey paper. I laid soft tones of blue- and green-greys over the distant trees, partly softening some of the pen drawing but retaining most of it in the nearer trees and rocks. Dark olive green with mid-sap green provided the foliage tints of the nearer trees on each side, and light sap green depicted the

sunlit banks. I used a few warm touches of yellow ochre and red-grey for the near slopes, and sharpened up the more distant trees with dark tones of sepia, which I also used to darken some of the near rocks on each side.

I put in the foaming water of the falls firmly with light and mid-tints of green-grey, with white highlights, and kept areas of the paper as mid-tones. The near pool of still water contained several of the above colours, particularly the dark sepia, and I laid these on with downward strokes to suggest reflections.

STILL WATER

There was an atmosphere of quiet stillness about *Brecfa Pool, near Brecon*, which attracted me by its simplicity. There was a lack of movement in the luminous sky, against which the distant contours of the Brecon Beacons presented their eternal sculpted forms and were mirrored in the still water. The dark trees and lower hills contrasted with the soft grey of the mountains, and their tones were echoed in the pool, with its edge curving towards the sunlit middle distance. The small farm buildings gave a vital scale to the whole.

My aim in *Stream near Dolgellau* (opposite) was to convey the transparency of the still water. As there was only a faint light from the sky filtering through the trees overhanging the stream, there were few reflections, which enabled me to look down into the near water to the rocky bed.

I laid on the basic colour with mid-tones of burnt umber and lighter touches of Vandyke brown and mid-olive green, rubbing them in firmly. Next, I drew in the darker forms of rocks which were visible on the bed of the stream and softened the edges by rubbing, but still retaining their forms.

A suggestion of ripples on the water's surface was created with a few soft sweeps of light blue-grey.

Brecfa Pool, near Brecon. 28 × 38 cm (11 × 15 in)

The dark, rocky slopes, particularly those on the right, provided a useful contrast with their reflections, and were drawn in firmly with dark tones of sepia. Varied touches of olive green, sap green and grey-green were applied for the soft, sunlit areas of foliage. A few broken touches of blue-grey produced the effect of light filtering through the trees, with light cerulean blue for the sparkle on the distant part of the stream.

Stream near Dolgellau. 28 × 38 cm (11 × 15 in)

Lastly, I drew in the tree trunks and branches, using dark sepia for those nearest and mid-blue-grey for the more distant ones.

Lechlade. 24 × 38 cm (9½ × 15 in)

This sketch of *Lechlade* on grey sugar paper depicts a quiet stretch of the upper Thames, where it flows gently between banks of overhanging willows and tall reeds. It made a simple but pleasing composition, with Lechlade church as a focal point. I drew in with a black fibre-tipped pen, which was particularly useful in defining the church. A rather subdued range of tones was appropriate for this tranquil scene.

6

SKIES

The sky is an important feature of the landscape, indicating the mood of the day, the weather and the direction of the wind. It is the source of light and forms the background against which we see the subject matter of our pictures: hills, mountains, buildings, trees and so on. John Constable was a painter who, probably more than any other, was intensely aware of skies. His studies in the Victoria and Albert Museum in London are gems of observation, and are accompanied by written notes giving not only the date on which the picture was painted, but also the time of day, the wind direction and other facts.

The flat landscape of eastern England is particularly dominated by the sky. This provides the opportunity to study the cloud formations with unrestricted views, and to become aware of the feeling of recession in both sky and landscape.

I tried to convey this feeling in *Lincolnshire landscape, September,*

Lincolnshire landscape, September.
24 × 37 cm (9½ × 14½ in)

a sketch on grey sugar paper, together with the varied light and shade across the broad acres of land. The warm tones of the cornfield and stubble reflected up into the sky, and the dark shades of the near trees contrasted with the smaller and softer trees in the distance.

Evening over the Severn Vale.
28 × 38 cm (11 × 15 in)

The warm evening shades of pink and ochre in *Evening over the Severn Vale* formed a contrast to the cool blue of the background and the distant Cotswold hills blending into the lower sky. I used the sharp contours of the farm buildings and the dark trees to give a greater luminosity to the sky. The cultivation lines in the field in the foreground lead the eye into the distance.

In the view shown in *Landscape near Brecon* (opposite) there was a softness over the distant

mountains, with the light coming from high in the sky and illuminating the middle distance. The shadow cast over the wooded slope to the left provided a contrast to the distant mountains.

I applied deep tones of purple- and green-greys, blending them together on the fine-grained sandpaper that I had selected. The lighter sides of the small trees in front stood out against this. I used the warmer darks of olive green and burnt umber for the nearer trees on the right, giving a

balancing tone to the wooded slope on the left. By contrast, the combined dark passages helped to give luminosity to the sky.

In *Breconshire landscape* (overleaf), to express the great cumulus clouds building up over the sharp contours of the Brecon Beacons, I chose pale tints of yellow ochre and Naples yellow for the light, against purple-greys, pale Prussian blue and cerulean blue. I put in the darker clouds, which were lower in the sky and not illuminated as well as the high cumulus, with blue-grey. These lower clouds were casting shadows over the landscape, and I attempted to capture these quickly, together with the lights, with tones of pale and deep olive green and with dark burnt umber for the large tree on the right. Lastly, I applied blue- and purple-greys in the middle distance against the soft blue-grey of the mountains.

Landscape near Brecon. 28 × 38 cm (11 × 15 in)

(Overleaf)
Breconshire landscape. 28 × 38 cm (11 × 15 in)

Ach-na-Aird, north-west Scotland.
28 × 38 cm (11 × 15 in)

Ach-na-Aird, north-west Scotland is a lovely spot dominated by the weather from the Atlantic – sometimes lashed by furious gales and at other times enjoying a tranquil calm. It was this latter mood which I was pleased to experience while working on this picture.

This wild country has provided me with many subjects in differing moods over the years. On this occasion I was attracted to the unity of land, water and sky. The shapes of the sands and water were echoed in the strata formation of the sky, as were the colours. There was a feeling of mystery in the soft, distant mountains, with the dark, clearly defined rock shapes on the shore in the foreground presenting a strong contrast.

I painted *Vale of Evesham, sunshine and showers* (opposite)

on a day of changing light and shade, giving the kind of conditions under which I like to work, although I knew that I must be prepared to make a quick dash for cover from sudden rainshowers. The strong light across the corn stubble formed a bright contrast to the dark shadowed trees and buildings, with the grey shapes of the distant Cotswolds softened by a retreating rainshower. The light cumulus clouds were partly obscured by the lower dark rain clouds.

I worked quickly on this sketch with my 'weather eye' open for the next shower. I kept everything simple in my attempt to capture the light across the field where the corn had been cut, for which I used pale yellow ochre. I shaped up the dark trees with purple- and green-greys, lightened with a few touches of mid-olive green. I kept the buildings small and unobtrusive with a light touch or two of pale ochre to show where the sunlight was catching them. The warm tones of burnt umber gave a shadowed foreground, and a few touches of dark and mid-olive green on the left suggested

Vale of Evesham, sunshine and showers. 28 × 38 cm (11 × 15 in)

a low hedgerow leading into the composition. The foreground tones combined to create a contrast to the sunlit area above, giving it more impact.

7

THE WINTER LANDSCAPE

I have always been attracted by the winter landscape because it offers so much to the painter, and I find it a great pity that so many people tend to write off this time of year as a 'closed season' for the artist. Adverse weather has to be expected during winter, but it is also possible during the summer months, when the average rainfall is often higher.

Views across the landscape are more open when seen through the bare branches of winter trees whose foliage obscures the scene in summer. The sun is never as high in the sky in winter, often resulting in long shadows and dramatic lighting effects. Colour, too, is plentiful, with the warm tints of leaves from the autumn remaining on the trees and hedgerows.

The distant landscape may assume lovely soft blue-grey tones as a result of a moist winter atmosphere; or a fall of snow may bring a completely new and fascinating world of changed tonal values, making the landscape appear lighter than the sky. It is an interesting experiment to place a small mirror on the snow, in a position where it reflects the sky, and to compare the tones of each. On a sunny day, the colour of the sky often reflects in cast shadows of a pale blue, contrasting with warm, sunlit areas.

Working out of doors in winter need not be too great a hardship if protective clothing is worn (particularly to guard against cold winds, which are the biggest problem), as well as waterproof shoes or boots. Working fairly quickly in pastel helps considerably too, and prevents one from becoming too cold as a result of sitting for a long period. If at all possible, try to choose a working position which is protected from the wind and in sunlight, where it can be surprisingly warm. There have been occasions when I have experienced snow falling on my paper as I worked, but as this was the dry, powdery kind, I was able to shake or blow it away before it melted and caused any damage.

Painting from a car is possible if it can be positioned in a suitable place, and, although obviously not a very satisfactory method of working, is preferable to missing a good picture. The most comfortable way of painting a snow scene is of course through the studio window, but such windows are not often strategically placed. If you do venture outside, it is always gratifying, having braved the elements, to come home with something worthwhile and to relish a little comfort!

DEMONSTRATION: WORCESTERSHIRE LANE

For this picture I chose an upright composition, which helped in portraying the height of the trees (particularly those on the left), and allowed me to leave an area where I could show the snow in the foreground. I selected a paper with a definite pink shade, making use

Stages 1 to 4 of *Worcestershire lane.*
32 × 25 cm (12½ × 10 in)
(See overleaf for method)

of this especially in the textured passages of the trees and in the foreground. The pink tint showed through, giving a warmish element to the work in contrast to the cooler passages, and is most noticeable in the snow-covered area in the foreground.

STAGE 1

I began with the sky, using light purple-grey, pale blue-grey and cerulean blue to cover part of the paper, and adding in pale ochre for a little warmth.

STAGE 2

I conveyed the cool, soft distance by rubbing in shades of a mid-toned blue-grey. I chose a darker blue-grey for the upper parts of the trees to the right, and dark purple-grey for the lower parts, merging this into dark and mid-toned olive green.

STAGE 3

I used the same pastels as a base tone for the left-hand trees, before drawing in the nearest large tree over this. Using the pastel on its side, I applied dark burnt umber to convey the masses of open twigs with a light pressure, allowing the underlying colours of both the paper and pastel to show through.

The finished painting of *Worcestershire lane*. 32 × 25 cm (12½ × 10 in)

STAGE 4

Next, I drew in the large tree more firmly with a dark tone of sepia and with lighter shades of warm grey and mid-olive green. I then began to introduce a tint of mid-ochre below the right-hand trees, repeating this in the lower areas of the trees to the left. I repeated the sky colours in the foreground and sketched in the figure.

THE FINISHED PAINTING

I dealt with the snow next, and here I put in the shadows with light tones of purple- and blue-greys, with a touch or two of light Prussian blue. I used warm grey for the lighter passages, and light lemon yellow for the highlights on the left-hand side of each wheelmark made by passing vehicles. The sun lighting these from a low level, and the long shadows cast across the foreground, were quite important in portraying the winter sunshine.

I drew in the man and his dog with Conté crayon, and applied cadmium red to his coat to give a bright spot of colour and to add interest and scale. Still working with the Conté, I firmed up the drawing of the trees, emphasizing the trunks and branches where necessary, and also the gate and fencing to the left. I drew in a few touches of mid-toned red-grey for the light trunks on the right, to make them stand out against the darker background. I put in some of the branches and posts to the left, and their green mossy parts,

with light green-grey, and added a suggestion of snow on the trees with light cerulean blue.

In this picture my aim was to capture the still atmosphere of a sunny winter's day, making use of tonal contrast and warm and cool colour. The pink tone of the paper was important, providing a warm contrast against the cool colours and giving unity to the whole picture.

The theme of *The Forest of Dean* (overleaf) was a sunny, snow-covered foreground fading into the mysterious depths of a forest. I created the background by blending light and mid-toned greys into the surface of the sandpaper which I had chosen. Against these colours, to left and right, I added tones of green- and purple-greys.

Next, I drew in the dark tree trunks with sepia, and used mid-cool grey for the softer trees. Light tints of Vandyke brown and mid-toned olive green supplied the lightest sunlit trunks. To create the sunlit effect and the texture in the foreground, I firmly laid on palest lemon yellow, with light tints of purple-grey and cerulean blue, without blending in, but retaining the warm shade of the paper.

To portray the warm shades of the old bracken and undergrowth showing through the snow, I firmly laid in burnt sienna and yellow ochre, laying the pastels on their sides and applying them in differing directional strokes. A few darker touches of sepia and olive green gave a little more tonal contrast to the light snow. Finally,

I carried some pale blue-grey into the shaded background to lead the eye into the forest.

I chose a deep-stone Ingres paper for *Credit River, Ontario* (opposite), which helped to set the tone of this rather low-key subject. Light tones of cerulean blue, burnt sienna and blue-grey in the sky, which I laid in first, helped to establish a background, against which I set the receding trees on the right. I used soft blue- and green-greys in the distance, moving forward with deep purple- and green-greys into mid-olive green, with some burnt umber added for further depth. I put in dark shades of grey- and olive-greens for the tall trees on the left.

I introduced a few warm touches of burnt sienna and yellow ochre to the woods on each side of the river in the nearer areas, suggesting foliage surviving from the autumn. The deep reflections were formed with dark tones of sepia and purple-grey, and were needed to create a contrast against the light snow on each bank. I added a few touches of pale grey to these to suggest ripples. I then drew in the dark tree trunks with deep tones of sepia and black Conté crayon, and indicated the lighter trunks with pale Vandyke brown. Pale blue-grey was reflected from the sky into the distant part of the river, with light yellow ochre for the sunlit areas of snow on each riverbank, and blue-grey for the shadows cast from the trees. Finally, I added a few highlights of white to the snow-covered area in the foreground and to the light passages. This created a useful echo of the light sky.

The Forest of Dean. 28 × 38 cm (11 × 15 in)

(Opposite) Credit River, Ontario. 35 × 25 cm (13½ × 10 in)

Cotswold winter. 25 × 28 cm
(10 × 15 in)

I carried out the quick study of *Cotswold winter* on sugar paper, with a few pastels over a black Conté crayon drawing. It was a bleak winter day, with a keen wind blowing as it so often does on those high Wolds. Working in the shelter of a stone wall, I attempted to capture the odd gleam of sunlight which at times managed to break through the grey, sullen sky. This is the kind of study which I find I can build on for further work in the comfort of the studio.

When I painted *Welsh border* (opposite, top), the snow was melting after what had been a heavy fall on the high hills near Kington in Herefordshire. The warm shades of the foreground faded into the cooler greys in the distance, with the stark, open branches of the trees presenting a helpful tonal contrast.

Snow in a Worcestershire lane (opposite) was a charcoal study of snow made on a day of sunshine, which cast shadows across the rutted, snow-covered roadway, with the added interest of the cottage and figures.

(Above)
Welsh border. 28 × 38 cm (11 × 15 in)

Snow in a Worcestershire lane.
30 × 42 cm (12 × 16½ in)

8

DISTANCE AND SPACE

The thirteenth-century artist Giotto is generally considered to be the first painter to have achieved depth and recession in his work: the illusion of a third dimension on a two-dimensional surface. The Dutch painters, such as Ruysdael and Hobbema captured it too in the seventeenth century when dealing with their flat landscape. As a landscape painter, it is one of my aims – certainly when dealing with an open view of land or sea – to convey this feeling of distance or space. For reasons of convenience in description we can generally divide a view into three areas: *foreground*, *middle distance* and *distance*.

In *View in the Black Mountains* (opposite) we can define the foreground of the composition as being the near area of large trees and sunlit field; the middle distance as the dark belt of trees and fields behind them; and the distance as the softer grey passages melting into the sky above.

There are several ways in which a feeling of recession can be

conveyed in a picture, of which scale is one. You will see that the trees in the foreground, particularly those to the right, are larger than those in the middle distance and distance. This is, of course, an obvious observation, but we need to make full use of its implications when painting the landscape.

Colour, too, can play its part in recession. It is obviously more positive on closer objects than on those further away, with the distance giving a cooler, blue-grey appearance. This is described as *aerial perspective*. You will notice in this picture that the nearer trees are a much more definite green than those in the mid-distance and distance, as is the nearer field. Darker tones, which give a contrast against the lights, play a significant part in the foreground. I used deep-toned burnt umber shades in the darkest passages in the trees. This is quite a warm colour, and contrasts with the cooler green-greys and blue-greys that I used for the mid-distance of the picture.

Other warm colours, such as those used in the foreground rough grass, are effective, and I have allowed the paper to show through here, which, with its warmish colour and texture, is also helpful.

I treated the distance in a much softer way, only using muted colours without strong contrast. The fields, woods and trees are smaller in scale and less clearly defined, with their forms blended into the sky to give a feeling of infinite distance and a sharp contrast to the foreground. The recession in the sky must not be forgotten, with the clouds which are near to us being larger and contrasting more in tone than those further away, until they lose their form altogether in the distance.

I have pleasant memories of the day in high summer when I painted this picture in the Black Mountains on the Welsh border. The views from their elevated slopes afford wonderful opportunities to experience distance and space and to translate them into paint.

View in the Black Mountains.
28 × 37 cm (11 × 14½ in)

In *Severn Valley* we have the areas of foreground, middle distance and distance tending to blend into each other. The foreground hill and trees swing down to the right, merging into the wooded rise in the mid-distance, which, in turn, slopes gradually left to join the plain below. This fades into the far distance, creating a good composition which tends to move the eye naturally through the picture from foreground to distance.

As in *View in the Black Mountains* on the previous page, the other elements of scale, colour and tone apply here in the trees, woods and fields. The horizon, although not quite lost, is soft and grey against the sky, in which the clouds grow smaller as they recede. The River Severn snaking away across the plain helps to lead the eye far away. I made this study from a position on one of the Shropshire hills so beloved of the Worcestershire poet and author, A.E. Housman.

Towards the Isle of Mull (opposite) shows a different setting, with a fine view across the sea to the mountains of Mull as seen from the rocky shore of Argyll in Scotland. For the foreground rocks I used dark and light warm colours, such as burnt umber, burnt sienna, and light and dark tones of olive green. I defined their shapes clearly with black Conté crayon, in contrast to the areas of land in the middle distance and the distant mountains.

I blended down the upper areas of grey sky to warmish tints of soft

Severn Valley. 24 × 37 cm (9½ × 14½ in)

burnt sienna and yellow ochre, making a muted background glow against which the distant mountain peaks of the Isle of Mull are visible. Note their soft treatment, with their forms dissolved into the mists creating a sense of mystery. This is in direct contrast to the clear shapes of the foreground, with the headlands on each side gradually receding and growing cooler and softer towards the distance. The green- and blue-grey tints of the sea from the darker, near areas, softening into the distance, also help in this way.

The yellow ochre light breaking through the clouds on the left, together with its reflection across the water, provides focal areas which attract the eye into the distance. This light is also echoed in the waves against the near rocks on the left.

Towards the Isle of Mull. 28 × 37 cm (11 × 14½ in)

I painted the study below, *Mountains near Dolgellau*, on a very hot July day. The slopes of Cader Idris (the highest peaks of which can be seen rearing their heads to the top right of the picture) rose above the valley. The whole of the far side of the valley was covered by a heat haze,

creating a softening effect, which helped me to treat the area simply.

Using cool tones of blue- and green-greys, I first shaped up the pattern of the fields. The whole of the foreground field was a warm colour resulting from the dry, hot weather, producing a helpful contrast against the cool distance. For this I used pale Vandyke brown with touches of light olive green, and the same colours in deeper tones for the shadowed foreground. The stone barn close to the big tree to the left was similar in colour, so I used light

and dark tints of Vandyke brown for this.

I blocked in the dark green trees firmly with deep shades of olive green and burnt umber, with a little mid-toned olive green for the lighter parts. I drew in the trees a little way behind these with deep purple-grey for those to the right of the barn, and dark green-grey for those to the left of the big tree. This entire dark area of trees provided a useful band of tone, separating the foreground and distance and creating a contrast with both.

Mountains near Dolgellau. 38 × 28 cm (15 × 11 in)

I put in the light clouds rising from behind the mountain with shades of pale ochre, soft tints of blue-grey and Prussian blue. A little work with a black Conté crayon on the fencing, barn and branches of the dark trees completed the study.

In *On the Black Mountains*, which is similar to the *Severn Valley* painting on page 68, I made use of the wooded slopes on the left of the composition to lead the eye down into the valley and up the other side. The trees in the foreground to the right prevent the eye from being swept out of the picture, allowing it to focus on the sunlit fields in the valley before moving out to the soft distance and the cumulus clouds above. In selecting this viewpoint I was able to convey the feeling of looking down from an elevated position. As I have said earlier, it always pays to have a quiet, contemplative look around before settling on a position from which to work.

On the Black Mountains. 28 × 38 cm (11 × 15 in)

A knowledge of the basic rules of perspective is needed by any artist wishing to convey a sense of a third dimension on a two-dimensional surface. In this chapter I have dealt with *aerial perspective*, the science of colour and tone in recession, but here I want to make a few comments

about *linear perspective*. Its rules do not require any artistic feeling: they are simply scientific and can be learned by anyone from the various books devoted to the subject. Ancient civilizations had a knowledge of linear perspective, but it was not until the early Renaissance period of the fourteenth century that any real treatises on the subject became available to us.

Here we have a charcoal study of a canal, bordered by reeds and flat meadows, with a few trees. I have superimposed lines which

converge to a vanishing point towards the centre. This illustrates the basic principles, as we see the canal becoming narrower as it recedes from us, as do the reeds on each bank together with their reflections. They appear to meet at a point on a level with our eyes, which is marked as the vanishing point. The trees become smaller as they recede, and the lines drawn along their tops also converge at the vanishing point. In effect, lines above eye level come down, while those below eye level rise to the vanishing point.

Charcoal study of a canal scene, showing the vanishing point and eye level.

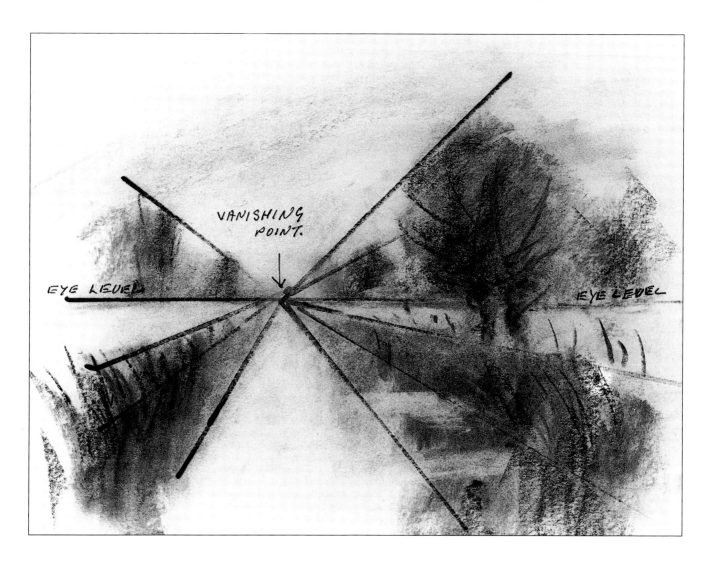

VANISHING POINT.

EYE LEVEL

EYE LEVEL

9

FIGURES AND ANIMALS

In the pictures and studies in this chapter we look at figures and animals, which 'support' the landscape rather than acting as principal features. They can play an important part in suggesting a feeling of scale, life and interest in a painting. I was careful to ensure in each case that they did not detract from the main interest of the work.

In *Figures on the beach*, a charcoal study, the figures help with scale and human interest and provide an upright element in the composition, contrasting with the horizontal planes of the rocks and waves on the shore. The two sketches overleaf, drawn in Conté crayon and charcoal, also demonstrate the usefulness of figures in providing scale and movement in a composition.

Figures on the beach. 25 × 42 cm (10 × 16½ in)

Charcoal and Conté crayon studies showing how figures add scale and movement to a drawing.

I painted *Green pastures near Brecon* on a lovely sunny day in high summer, in a pastoral valley under the peaks of the Brecon Beacons. The cows played an important part in the composition by providing some interest in the foreground field, which would have been rather empty without them. Fortunately they were there grazing peacefully in the green

Green pastures near Brecon.
28 × 38 cm (11 × 15 in)

meadow, so I simply made use of them to complete the scene; otherwise I would have used some animals from my sketchbooks on my return home.

I included the two figures in *Children in the wood, spring* (opposite) as I felt that they were needed to complete the atmosphere of a bright sunny morning in spring. With a feeling of new life and growth in the trees and flowers, and in the sunlight of early morning, children seemed to add the appropriate final touch.

Whenever I am working out of doors and someone walks into the scene, I quickly draw them in if possible, because they are usually in keeping with the picture. If the subject contains boats, for instance, there is usually someone pulling on a rope or carrying out some other activity which seems natural. People working in the fields may also be appropriate to a landscape scene.

I find it useful to be able to refer to my sketchbook at times for single figures or groups of people. Good places to make such studies are railway and bus depots or airports, where people gather in groups or stand about, making good models. Using a sketchbook in such places, where people often sit reading or writing, need not be too obvious an activity.

My sketch of *Cattle in a stream* was made on a hot summer's day when the cows were seeking the coolness of the stream. Their warm, burnt sienna shades contrasted well with the greens behind. This kind of study could be built up to a completed picture, and in order to help with this, I made some further reference drawings of the cows with a biro (see overleaf).

(Opposite)
Children in the wood, spring.
32×25 cm $(12\frac{1}{2} \times 10$ in$)$

Cattle in a stream. 25×38 cm
$(10 \times 15$ in$)$

Quick reference sketches made in biro.

In *Cattle in the snow, Castlemorton* I rubbed a mid-grey pastel on to cartridge paper to suggest the soft tones of the background willows, and drew in the near trees and the cattle with Conté crayon. I rubbed in grey pastel for the shadowed foreground, and lifted out the lights with a putty eraser.

Cattle in the snow, Castlemorton.
29 × 42 cm (11½ × 16½ in)

10

BUILDINGS

I am always attracted by a building which looks as if it has grown up naturally from its surroundings. This is usually the case when it has been built from local stone quarried nearby, such as Welsh slate or Cotswold stone. With the former, man has often brightened it with a little white paint, thus highlighting an otherwise rather sombre mountainside.

I sketch and paint buildings in many different parts of the country, and often find myself comparing the different styles, from the timber-framed dwellings of pastoral landscapes to the solid stone structures on hills and mountains. I wonder, too, why they were built in certain positions – often not on the site that I would have chosen, with windows looking out on a fine view, but set behind a great rocky crag. Perhaps the question is answered for me when I go there on a bleak winter's day of wind and rain, and realize that the crag which obscures the view is in fact there to provide much-needed shelter.

I am often interested by the reasons for a building being sited in this way, and the use which has also been made, at times, of a natural feature such as a great outcrop of rock, which may have been incorporated into a part of a wall, adding to the appearance of the building having grown out of the landscape itself.

In the scene shown in my *Welsh farm* painting (overleaf), the surrounding mountains give shelter from most directions, but the valley is open to the sea and the strong westerly gales, which at times create other problems. All these elements tend to relate the farm to its natural setting, which I have tried to convey in my painting.

The farm nestles beside the river in its sheltering valley, making a natural composition with both mountains and river leading the eye in. I painted this picture on a fine morning in late summer with mists still lingering in the valley.

The blue-grey tones of the background mountains gave a feeling of recession, fading away into a soft distance, and the dark green-grey trees behind the farm made a useful contrast against the lighter tones of the farmhouse. The sun breaking through the mist was casting shadows across the foreground from trees bordering the river. The large tree on the right made a useful dark against the mountains behind, and its contrast to the size of the other trees added to the feeling of recession.

The cool blue sky and pale grey distant mountains reflected in the water provided a helpful contrast to the foreground greens. In the same context, the warm ochre tints in the sky echoed the colours of the farm buildings and created a foil to the cool tints of the sky and mountains.

I applied Conté crayon with its firm point to draw in, emphasizing the shapes of the farm buildings together with the trunks and branches of the near right-hand tree, the gate and the fencing posts.

(Overleaf)
Welsh farm. 28 × 38 cm (11 × 15 in)

I thought this *Carmarthenshire farmstead* a typical mountain farm, looking as if it had grown up on the mountainside and nestling on the slopes which gave it shelter. I made a rough exploratory sketch, attempting to capture its setting as much as anything else.

Carmarthenshire farmstead.
24 × 37 cm (9½ × 14½ in)

As will be apparent, I did not really know quite how to tackle this scene, especially when I came to the foreground area. Sketching from nature can be a humbling experience (as Constable told us), and this gave me some measure of comfort in my efforts. This is the kind of study which I often make quickly on the spot and which will probably be useful at some later time in the studio.

With regard to the foreground trees, I felt that if I were to put them in as strongly as they actually appeared, they would dominate the subject entirely and take away the importance of the farm, which was the true motif.

I drew in on sugar paper, using Conté crayon on its side as well as with the point, and added a little pastel for a suggestion of colour.

The next painting, shown opposite, is entitled *Evening light, Easdale Island*. This island, which lies off the Argyll coast of western Scotland in the Firth of Lorne, was a settlement of people who lived by quarrying the local slate and by fishing. A freak storm combined with a high tide in 1881 washed over the island, flooding the open-cast mines which were never

operated again. Fortunately no lives were lost, and the community returned as if in defiance of the elements, with their only communication with the mainland being a small motorboat ferry which plys across the narrow strip of water.

I was attracted to the subject by the light towards the end of the day, which was making a sharp contrast behind the dark shapes of the rocks and buildings. These played an important part in the composition, providing a focal area against the light sky and the blue-grey shape of the island of Scarba rising from the open sea beyond. The light from the sky reflected in the water leads the eye from the foreground rocks towards the buildings.

I kept the upper part of the sky fairly subdued in tone, giving a contrast to the light area below, behind the buildings. Once again

Evening light, Easdale Island.
28 × 38 cm (11 × 15 in)

I made use of a black Conté crayon to emphasize the sharp contours of the houses and rocks, and chose warm tints of umbers and ochres for the foreground shore.

It was towards evening when I was attracted to the impressive silhouetted shapes of the *Houses of Parliament*, set against a luminous sky. I drew in with Conté crayon and worked over it with shades of blue- and red-grey pastels, finally sharpening up the outlines with biro. The barges provided a nice tonal contrast to the light reflections in the river.

The buildings in *Farm in Gwynedd, north Wales* (opposite, top) gave the appearance of snuggling down among the trees in

Houses of Parliament. 23 × 32 cm (9 × 12½ in)

their sheltered valley at the foot of the mountains. I chose a mid-grey-toned Ingres paper for my picture, which helped me to create the impression of the soft mountain background and the deep green-grey of the trees behind the farm. It was important not to make these areas too strong and thereby dominate the composition.

I used stronger tones for the shadowed parts of the farm and nearer trees, which, together with the lights on each, created a contrast and brought them forward. I found the stone wall leading in from the foreground on the left very useful as a powerful

dark passage. Firm drawing with a Conté crayon helped to sharpen up the contours of the buildings and stone wall, and the light coming from high in the sky gave the atmosphere of a warm afternoon in late summer.

From Westminster Bridge (opposite, bottom) was a similar subject to *Houses of Parliament*, and I painted it looking across the River Thames towards Westminster. There was a warm glow in the sky, with the buildings and Lambeth bridge in silhouette, and I treated these in the same way as the *Houses of Parliament* sketch.

(Above)
Farm in Gwynedd, north Wales.
25 × 35 cm (10 × 13½ in)

From Westminster Bridge. 23 × 32 cm
(9 × 12½ in)

Cotswold village. 32 × 25 cm
($12\frac{1}{2}$ × 15 in)

I chose a stone-coloured paper for *Cotswold village* (opposite) and made use of this to represent the natural colour of the Cotswold stone. I drew in with black Conté crayon, followed by pale Prussian blue pastel for the sky, which immediately set the cool contrast against the warm colour of the buildings.

I completed the study with the shadowed foreground below the sunlit area, and added a few cool greys and blues for the reflected light in the windows. The figures added a sense of scale and some bright colour.

Ludlow Castle has always been a favourite subject of mine, standing as it has done down the centuries, with its massive keep dating from the time of Henry I. Could it but speak, it could tell many tales of ferocious battles, treachery and intrigue. It stands on its hill like a protective sentinel, guarding the town and the peaceful Shropshire landscape, with the sparkling waters of the River Teme flowing below.

Ludlow Castle. 23 × 32 cm (9 × 12½ in)

I have on another occasion painted the castle with its towers sunlit against storm clouds, but this time I saw it dark and solid against a luminous sky. The sunlit passage of the middle distance created a contrast to the shadowed castle and dark foreground, while the dark storm cloud high in the sky gave value to the light below.

11

TREES

I selected a piece of stone-grey Canson paper for my *Winter tree study*, an example of the technique used to deal with a bare winter tree. With a pale tint of French ultramarine, and holding the pastel flat on the paper, I laid in the sky, not pressing firmly but just tinting the paper. Next, I dragged a dark sepia stick rather firmly across the paper over the first colour, taking the strokes inward towards the centre of the tree. This suggested the masses of bare twigs, which I was able to vary by using more pressure in some passages than in others. I completed the study with the sepia pastel, used on its edge and applied more firmly with bold strokes to indicate the dark trunk and branches.

Winter tree study. 37 × 27 cm (14½ × 10 in)

This study of *Cotswold lane, spring* is similar to *Cotswold lane, winter sunshine* (overleaf), with its play of sunlight and shadow across the roadway and grass verges bordered by trees. I painted this during the month of May when the wild cow parsley brightened up the country lanes.

The trees had not yet come into full leaf, so I was able to see the cool tones of those in the distance. Using a broad fibre-tipped pen

Cotswold lane, spring. 25 × 32 cm (10 × 12½ in)

I drew in the main shapes, paying particular attention to the trees with their strongly toned trunks and branches. This provided a strong basic drawing which could be covered with pastel if necessary. The light tones of the cow parsley with its sunshine and shadow gave a highlight in the foreground.

While driving over the Cotswolds on a winter's day, I began to wonder if I had mistaken the date. Could it be April instead of January? The sunshine and mild air certainly seemed to relate more to spring than winter. Having viewed a likely subject I decided to stay and enjoy the weather while sketching.

Cotswold lane, winter sunshine.
25 × 32 cm (10 × 12½ in)

The result, shown in *Cotswold lane, winter sunshine*, was an example of the advantage which I always maintain applies in being able to see through the bare branches of winter trees. The distant hill gave depth and recession, and the sunlight across the roadway and grass verges offered a useful area of bright colour which contrasted with the cooler, softer distance. I quickly drew in the figure which appeared over the rise in the road.

In *Winter trees and Malvern hills* the warm umber and ochre shades in the foreground trees on each side of the composition created a useful contrast against the cool blue-greys of the background hills. The buildings in the middle distance helped to convey scale, and the bright sunlight playing on them behind the dark of the near trees created liveliness. The lights in the sky reflected in the foreground stream acted as a link between the two foreground tree groups.

Winter trees and Malvern hills.
28 × 38 cm (11 × 15 in)

Willows near Tewkesbury. 28 × 38 cm
(11 × 15 in)

I was attracted to the strong,
dark shapes of the trees in *Willows
near Tewkesbury*, and so I drew in
firmly, having first painted the pale
blue and the blue-greys of the
distant hills. These were reflected
in the stream and gave a fine lead
into the picture.

My study of *Watermeadows
near Tewkesbury* (opposite, top)
was carried out on a spot near to

the one at which I painted *Willows
near Tewkesbury*, and the right-
hand trees feature in both. A lovely
warm mass of twigs and branches
in this group was lit by the winter
sunlight, while a cloud shadow
cast across the foreground
provided a helpful contrast.

I used the soft greys of the
distance as a foil to the nearer
warm tones of the trees and
shadowed foreground. The cows
were a feature of interest in what
could have been a rather empty
space.

(Above)
Watermeadows near Tewkesbury.
28 × 38 cm (11 × 15 in)

Cotswold elms shows two of the
last of these stately trees rising
above the stumps of their fallen
comrades, the victims of Dutch
Elm disease. I was glad to be able
to draw them.

Cotswold elms. 24 × 37 cm
(9½ × 14½ in)

My final sketch for this chapter, *Tree in winter*, was carried out fairly rapidly in charcoal. The figures of the man and his dog, and the fence to the right of the tree, create points of interest and give a sense of scale.

Tree in winter. 42 × 20 cm (16½ × 8 in)

12

MOOD

Mood plays a very important part in landscape painting, whether it is a convincing feeling of season, weather, space, distance or light. A plain rendering of topographically cold facts, without this extra dimension, can leave the viewer unmoved.

Whenever memory takes me back to a place, it is not so much the topographical features that come to mind, but the season, weather or time of day. I may recall a lovely landscape, with beautifully formed mountains or trees, but they are less significant in themselves than the *conditions* under which I experienced the scene, proving that the greatest impact that it made on me was one of mood.

I suppose it is for this reason that I find myself in sympathy with the Impressionists, that group of painters generally considered to represent the greatest art movement since the Renaissance. Mood and atmosphere were their actual subjects, although, of course, they needed to make use of a landscape as a setting which was

kept subservient to this theme. One of their leaders, Claude Monet (1840–1926), comes to mind, particularly with his 'series paintings' in which he created a succession of studies of Rouen Cathedral, views on the Seine, haystacks and poplar trees, all under the day's changing light and atmosphere.

In the same way, I would like to relate my own experiences in attempting to capture passing moods. I often work with groups of students on the shore of Tal-y-Llyn, a lovely lake nestling in a valley below some of the impressive mountains of north Wales. In such a setting, sudden changes of weather are experienced, giving one the opportunity to capture the effects of the kind of storm that sends one leaping for cover.

I have studied and sketched this lake under many different moods. Fertile green slopes rise from its shores, with woods of oak and birch covering the lower slopes and rising through areas of scree to rocky outcrops, culminating in the

high, rearing head of Cader Idris.

The mood changes through the passing seasons, when the mountain slopes are gradually released from winter's grip and snow gives way to the gentle tones of spring. The calm, warm days of high summer reveal the woods clothed in heavy greens, which reflect in the still waters. Summer merges imperceptibly into the glorious autumn season, with its riot of colour and mellow sunshine, until once more the chill winds charged with snow bring winter again. I love this pageant that nature provides for us through the passing seasons.

It is not only in winter that a sudden storm can vent its fury across the valley, and whip up the still waters of the lake, shattering its still reflections into driven waves. It was just such an experience that I attempted to express in the following studies of a storm which developed suddenly on a day in high summer when the lake was as smooth as a mirror, reflecting a reverse image of the mountains and woods.

STORM OVER TAL-Y-LLYN

I carried out the following four studies to illustrate the stages of this storm as it passed over the lake. The studies demonstrate once again the spontaneous use of pastels, showing how they can be used to capture the passing moods of nature and provide the materials for building up convincing pictures in the studio. I use the expression 'convincing pictures' with significance, as I maintain that we need to experience nature in all her moods before we can convey our understanding to others.

STUDY 1

A storm had just passed over and I was able to work quickly on sugar paper, attempting to capture the effect of the rain cloud which

partly obscured the mountains on the far shore of the lake. I suggested the mountain shapes in the centre with soft greys, and shaped up the peaks on the left with darker tones of blue-grey. I also added a few touches of pale ochre where the light was beginning to break through and reflect on the lake. Quick touches of mid- and dark tones of burnt umber vaguely suggested the foreground bushes and rocks. This was all that I had time for before I tackled the next stage.

STUDY 2

The rain cloud which had nearly obscured the mountain had now moved further to the right, casting its shadow, but with some light still breaking through beneath it. I quickly blocked in the distant right-hand mountain, and the cloud above it, using a mid-toned

blue-grey and pale yellow ochre for the light showing through and for the distant part of the lake.

The left-hand slopes were not much changed, although with a clearer atmosphere the lower area appeared greener, which I put in with a dark olive. As before, I applied dark blue-grey above this and to the lower slopes on the right. Middle tones of blue-grey gave me the surface of the lake, and I used the previous tones of mid- and dark burnt umber to indicate the foreground.

STUDY 3

The main storm cloud had now moved yet further away, but this time to the left, and had risen to cast its shadow over the furthest mountain slopes. There was more light in the sky beyond the dark cloud, with some patches of blue breaking through. More light – the result of a clearer sky following the storm – was also flooding on to the lake and the lower slopes above it, revealing more of the woods and fields.

I used many of the same pastels as before, with dark blue-grey supplying the whole range of distant mountains. I brought pale Prussian blue, light yellow ochre and a little white into use for the sky below the mid-blue-grey of the storm cloud and for the reflections in the lake. I applied green-greys in light, middle and dark tints for the

Study 1 of *Storm over Tal-y-Llyn.*
25 × 37 cm (10 × 14½ in)

lower mountain slopes, and indicated sunny patches with light lizard green. The near mountain slopes on the left were mid-sap green, with dark olive for the trees at the base. Dark sepia gave the foreground colour.

(Right)
Study 2 of *Storm over Tal-y-Llyn.*
25 × 37 cm (10 × 14½ in)

(Below)
Study 3 of *Storm over Tal-y-Llyn.*
25 × 37 cm (10 × 14½ in)

STUDY 4

For this sketch I moved my position to obtain a view a little further back. I had time to do this, as the storm had passed away into the distance leaving a more serene mood and a pleasant summer day to enjoy painting. The same pastels were used for this study as for the previous three.

I should mention that the mid-grey tint of the sugar paper played a vital part in all these sketches, as I was able to leave parts untouched by pastel to play their role in the

Study 4 of *Storm over Tal-y-Llyn*.
25 × 37 cm (10 × 14½ in)

tonal scheme. These studies are presented exactly as I produced them, with little topographical detail or precision.

There was a feeling of tranquil calm about the scene in *Evening over the loch* (opposite, top), and I chose a deep-stone Ingres paper which helped to set the tonal key. A mist was rising, softening the distant contours of the mountains.

I began by rubbing soft tones of blue-grey and pale burnt sienna for the sky, and a slightly darker tint of blue-grey for the distant hills, into the surface of the dark paper. I gradually introduced darker shades of grey, blending with

dark autumn brown into black compressed charcoal for the nearest darks. These tones were brought down and rubbed into the water area to create reflections.

I drew in the sharp contours of the buildings with black Conté crayon, to give a focal point and scale, followed by the highlights of light ochre and their reflections. The dark autumn-brown tones of the left foreground contrasted with the light reflections in the water, and, together with the middle-distant headland, balanced the dark slopes on the right.

I painted *Misty morning on the Usk* (opposite, bottom) in winter, with soft sunlight filtering through

(Above)
Evening over the loch. 25 × 35 cm
(10 × 14 in)

mists rising from the River Usk in
south Wales. I was attracted by the
dark tones of the near trees
contrasting with the vague shapes
behind, particularly those against
the lightest part of the sky. I was
also intrigued by the sky's
reflection in the water, which
provided a focal point. A few soft
greens, one or two greys, pale
yellow ochre and dark sepia were
all that I needed for this quiet
mood study.

Misty morning on the Usk. 24 × 32 cm
(9½ × 12½ in)

99

Spring showers, Worcester. 37 × 51 cm
(14½ × 20 in)

The cathedral and other
buildings in *Spring showers,
Worcester* were seen in an almost
theatrical light against the
background of storm clouds. The
storm, having passed over, had
washed the landscape, leaving it
clean and fresh. To complete the
operation, nature had brought out
a gentle breeze which stirred the
trees in front of the cathedral and
dried them in spring sunshine.

I treated architectural details
simply with light shades of Naples
yellow and Vandyke brown
against the blue-grey of the lower
sky. I applied greens, comprising
three shades of olive, with dark
green-grey and a range of light and
mid-sap greens, for the sunlit trees
and foreground meadow, and
brought in tones of blue- and
green-greys to form the shadowed
passages below and between the
buildings. I drew in the cows with
light and dark burnt sienna, and
used dark sepia to strengthen the
trunks and branches of the nearest
tree on each side. The light clouds,
high in the sky, echoed the pale
Naples yellow of the cathedral.

TONAL IMPRESSIONS

I often think it a pity that many students go out on painting trips with a vision of triumphantly bringing back at least one complete and successful picture on each occasion, instead of spending time exploring tonal relationships, composition, form and so on. The following pictures are quick impressions, in which I attempted to capture some of the tonal and colour effects which often pass so swiftly.

The first of these is shown in *Herefordshire lane, early summer.*

On a bright day in May, the milky-white tones of the wild cow parsley appeared almost luminous against the surrounding greens of the verges and hedgerows. Ignoring detail, I blocked in the main dark trees, with tones of olive green for the nearest and dark green-grey for the one behind, against the natural grey of the Ingres paper which represented the sky.

I used mid-tints of olive and sap greens for the hedgerows and verges, contrasting with pale Naples yellow and cerulean blue for the cow parsley. I laid in light and mid-tints of red-grey for the road, and added autumn brown for the darks in the trees and blue-grey for the distance. Lastly, I brought in Conté crayon for the telegraph posts and road edges. I could have developed the picture further on this basis, but I found it important to go for the essentials of the subject, knowing that they might have eluded me had I attempted anything further.

Herefordshire lane, early summer.
25×32 cm ($10 \times 12\frac{1}{2}$ in)

(Above)
The Cuillins, Isle of Skye. 25 × 32 cm
(10 × 12½ in)

The serrated peaks of the mountains appeared during a break in the clouds and formed the focal point of the study of *The Cuillins, Isle of Skye.* The sunlight brought out the forms of the hills below the mountains and sparkled on the distant water of the loch. I kept the foreground of water and rocky shore broad in treatment, the colours being mainly greys, both warm and cool, with darks of autumn brown and olive green.

My final 'impression' is shown in *Severn floods and Malvern hills.* Floodwater, like snow, can produce dramatic effects in the landscape. In either case tonal relationships are changed, with water reflecting light from the sky in areas which would normally be darker in tone. Here, the light from a bright day sparkled on the floodwaters covering the meadows by the River Severn. The winter trees and distance made a sharp contrast against these, with the range of the Malvern hills adding their fine contours. This study provided me with material for an Imperial-sized picture.

Severn floods and Malvern hills.
24 × 32 cm (9½ × 12½ in)

13

LIGHT AND SHADE

Light and shade provide the means of creating drama and impact in a picture, giving life and vigour to the subject. The painters Carravagio (1573–1610) and Joseph Wright of Derby (1734–97) come to mind, together with the Impressionists, as great masters of light and drama, and a study of their work can be of considerable help in realizing the significance of these elements.

The ability of such techniques to carry conviction calls for a confident and bold approach on the part of the artist. Tonal relationships play a vital part in our considerations when dealing with these matters, and the use of exploratory studies – particularly in charcoal – can be a help, as I have illustrated in other chapters.

I came across the subject in *Clearing storm, Loch Creran, Argyll* as I was driving along the shore of the loch on a day of uncertain early spring weather. I was initially attracted by some lovely shades of light falling on the mountains across the loch. I decided that here was a subject,

but before I could settle down in a good position from which to work, a sudden change in the weather brought clouds down over the mountains and rain began to sweep across the loch, obliterating everything from view.

I was able to park the car in a convenient layby from which I could at least see the rocks by the shore. As this was a sudden

onslaught by the weather I hoped for an equally sudden improvement. Fortunately I did not have long to wait before the sun began to break through the storm clouds, producing some

---

Charcoal study of *Clearing storm, Loch Creran, Argyll.*

Clearing storm, Loch Creran, Argyll.
28 × 38 cm (11 × 15 in)

lovely soft tones on the lower slopes of the mountains and giving light reflections in the waters of the loch.

I felt that it would be rather risky to settle down to work outside, but, luckily, as the weather began to clear, I realized that I had quite a good view from the car and set about trying to capture the scene. As light and shade were obviously very important in this subject, a charcoal study (shown on the previous page) was a help in exploring the tonal relationships, and I completed this very quickly before conditions changed again.

The darker tone of the mountain slope on the left made a dramatic contrast against the light sky behind, together with the reflections of both in the water. The soft tones of the distant mountains gradually became darker towards the foreground. The dark, rocky shore made a strong base to the composition. In the finished picture (above), colour played a secondary role, with soft, cool greys in the distance and warmer (but soft) tints in the lighter passages of the right-hand mountain slopes and warm, dark shades in the foreground.

The light clouds made a contrast between the distant mountains and dark clouds above in *A bright interval* (opposite, top). This was echoed in the middle distance with the light from the break in the sky illuminating the hillside and contrasting with the dark trees. I made good use of these contrasting tones by bringing the lights sharply up to the darks, which gave vigour and impact to the subject.

(Above) A bright interval. 28 × 38 cm
(11 × 15 in)

In *Evening light*, a charcoal and
fibre-tipped-pen study, I explored
the use of tonal contrast from the
white of the cartridge paper to the
intense black produced by the
fibre-tipped pen. I drew in first
with the pen, producing firm
contours and solid forms by
shading in the darks. This dried
very quickly, allowing me to lay
charcoal over the drawing, using a
piece about an inch long, rubbing

Evening light. 27 × 35 cm (10½ × 14 in)

it in where necessary and then lifting out with a putty eraser to produce the light areas.

This study makes apparent the fact that where there is a strong tonal contrast the eye will tend to

be attracted to it. The strongest contrast which can be achieved is, of course, black and white, and this can be used for parts of a composition which need to be clearly seen, and which command our immediate attention. This kind of contrast can be used as a focal point, with other related passages in support. It is a good idea to keep strong tonal contrasts away from the edges of a picture, as they tend to make the eye drift out of the work.

With the last of the day's light fading behind the mountains and reflecting in the water, there was a calm stillness over the scene below in *Evening on the loch*. This study was dependent on a range of tones, from the highest light in the sky (for which I used white), to the intense black of compressed charcoal for the darkest mountains. I chose a deep-stone paper for this study, which remained uncovered in varying degrees throughout the picture and

Evening on the loch. 25 × 32 cm (10 × 12½ in)

gave me considerable help as I worked.

The only other colours that I used were deep purple-grey for the distant mountain peaks in the centre, a middle shade of burnt sienna together with light yellow ochre for the lights and their reflections, and some dark tones of sepia for the mountain shapes to add a little warmth. The sharp edges of the left-hand shoreline, drawn in firmly with the compressed charcoal, formed a useful contrast and a repetition of the light and dark of the skyline above.

DEMONSTRATION: AFON CADER, NORTH WALES

There is a secluded valley nestling under the steep slopes of Cader Idris, along which a dashing stream cascades over its rocky bed, at times pausing to gather its clear waters into still, shady pools beneath sheltering ash, birch or beech trees. This is the Afon Cader, which takes its name from the mountain which gave it birth.

It was very pleasant on a hot summer day to seek shade under

Charcoal study of *Afon Cader, north Wales.*

the overhanging trees beside the chattering stream. I found a convenient boulder on which to sit and another on which to set out my pastels. I needed, first of all, to explore the general composition and tonal relationships before embarking on a full colour study, so I quickly worked these out in a charcoal sketch, rubbing in for soft passages and lifting out areas with a putty eraser for the lights.

107

STAGE 1

I began to lay in the distant background tones on sandpaper, with green-grey pastel rubbed in with a piece of card and light blue-grey for the sky showing through in the upper part, with a darker blue-grey lower down to the right. I retained the paper untouched for the lower part, except for a touch of blue-grey on the right to suggest water.

STAGE 2

Next, I worked in dark olive green on each side of the background

and on the bank in the right foreground, leaving the centre green-grey. With a dark sepia to set the tone, I began to draw in the tree trunks on the right and suggested the darks of the boulders below them and to the left. I indicated the light in the mid-distance to the left and right of the stream with pale red-grey (this was similar to the tone of the paper) but needed to work it up afterwards to lighten it.

STAGE 3

I continued to draw in firmly the dark tree trunks and the shaded

boulders below, leaving the paper untouched for the water area, except for a suggestion of green-grey. I then added a lighter olive green to the dark areas of foliage to both right and left, breaking them up to indicate the sunlight filtering through.

THE FINISHED PAINTING

Finally, I concentrated on the foreground, which consisted of the water flowing from my left between the dark, shadowed boulders and away into the distance. Although the whole of the foreground area was in shade, the water was mostly light as it was partly reflecting the sky and breaking into spray over the rocks. This contrast of light and shade gave me the opportunity of some lively interest in this area. I shaped up the rocks with dark shades of sepia and green-grey, and used a mid-toned olive green for lighter,

Stages 1 to 3 of *Afon Cader, north Wales*. Each 14×19 cm ($5\frac{1}{2} \times 7\frac{1}{2}$ in)

mossy parts. Dark and mid-tints of green-grey provided the tones of the water, together with a pale blue-grey for the lightest passages.

Next, I dealt with the sunny area on each side of the stream in the middle distance with a light Vandyke brown, and drew in the tree trunks on the left against the darker foliage behind with a mid-toned green-grey. I shaped up the other middle-distance trees to the right with a soft warm grey.

This more or less completed the picture, but as I was feeling rather cramped, having been sitting and concentrating for some time, I decided to take a walk to stretch my legs. I usually take a break like this as it enables me to return and view the work with a fresh eye, so that I am better able to see any weakness and how to apply the vital finishing touches. It is so easy to over-work a picture, and if you do not pause and take stock in this way, faults can develop of which you may not be aware until it is too late.

I pulled the picture together by shaping up the foliage in the upper area, introducing more light with pale tones of sap and olive greens. I added a little more drawing to the trunks and branches and brought in some light French ultramarine to suggest areas of bright sky showing through the leaves.

It may appear that I used white in the lightest parts of the picture (i.e., the breaking water over the foreground rocks and the light banks beyond), but this is not so; it is, rather, that the tonal value of the darks makes these passages appear lighter by contrast. I use very little white pastel in my colour work as I feel that over-using it can produce a chalky

_____

The finished painting of *Afon Cader, north Wales*. 28 × 38 cm (11 × 15 in)

effect. In preference, I favour the lightest tints of Naples yellow, yellow ochre or lemon yellow. As for the tonal relationships in the picture, I derived, as usual, great help from my exploratory charcoal sketch.

As I paused and walked around before completing my first picture of this subject, I came upon the same view in reverse, shown here. You may recognize some of the same features in each picture, such as the bent tree to the left of centre in each case. In the second view, there was more light on the banks of the stream and in the foreground, the greens here (olive and sap greens) being a repetition of those used in the foliage above.

I laid in the colours of the boulders with cool, mid-toned greys emphasized with dark sepia. The water area comprised three tints of green-grey (dark, mid- and light) and I put in the highlights on the rocks with light Vandyke brown. Some dark purple-grey in the middle distance, to the left of the bent tree, gave a useful contrast behind the boulders and grass.

I painted this second picture in very much the same way as the first, by laying in the background with green-greys for the darkest trees, and rubbing these in before working over with olive and sap greens, each in light, mid- and dark tints, but left unrubbed. Pale blue-grey suggested light from the sky breaking through the foliage. The light had, of course, changed somewhat by the time I began the second picture, as you can tell by the bent tree near the centre, which is in shadow in the first picture and light in the second. With subjects like this, where numerous trees are involved, I do not paint each individual tree, but select and include those of the most interesting shape or character. I select and adjust groups of trees in the same way.

The second version of this painting was not intended to be a reverse copy of the first; I simply felt that – with a different viewpoint and a changed light – there was potential for another picture. A strength and stability was given to the composition by the deep-toned trees to the left, with their trunks and branches drawn in with sepia and foliage of dark olive green with a little sepia added.

Reverse view of *Afon Cader, north Wales*. 28 × 38 cm (11 × 15 in)

14

NOCTURNES

I am fascinated by nocturnal subjects. They often suggest a wonderful atmosphere of mystery, whereas the same scene observed in the clear light of day can appear quite mundane. Street scenes at night, illuminated by shop lights and lamps (especially when trees are included) appeal greatly to me – even more so when the street is wet with rain and reflects the light and colour.

We often fail to see ordinary streets as subjects, and only become aware of them when compelled to wait perhaps at a bus stop or in a traffic queue. There is little we can do on such occasions, except to take a searching look, trying to impress the subject on our mind, and, as soon as possible on returning home, to make some quick studies and notes from which to build up a subject. It can be helpful to return to the same subject during daylight to record

some of the details, when it will probably not appear at all interesting and you will wonder why it impressed you earlier. This proves, of course, that it was the *conditions* under which you saw it – in effect, the light – which gave the scene its appeal.

Some drawings, carried out in soft pencil and giving basic topographical details, can be of assistance in composing the subject, but these must only be used to *support* the main theme. The following nocturne was the result of my experience in observing such effects, and does not represent an actual scene – it is a combination of memory impressions.

Charcoal sketch of *Street nocturne.*

DEMONSTRATION: STREET NOCTURNE

In my initial charcoal study (opposite) I attempted to set down an impression of the essentials of my remembered subject. I rubbed a mid-tone of the charcoal over a sheet of cartridge paper and laid in the darks with compressed charcoal and Conté crayon. I lifted out the lights with a soft putty eraser.

STAGE 1

The first painting stage was to make a pastel sketch using the charcoal study as reference. I chose a mid-grey sugar paper and, in addition to charcoal, began to introduce colour with pastel, first of all establishing the sky with a darkish blue-grey. I then placed the dark tones of the silhouetted buildings against this with charcoal. Bright pastels of yellow ochre and cadmium red laid on the otherwise untouched paper gave the effect of a brightly lit area. I then drew in the dark trees and figures against the light with black Conté crayon. I felt now, without having made any attempt at topographical exactitude, that I had worked out enough of my problems to enable me to proceed to the final stage.

Stage 1: charcoal and pastel sketch of *Street nocturne.* 16 × 21 cm ($6\frac{1}{2}$ × $8\frac{1}{2}$ in)

THE FINISHED PAINTING

I chose a sheet of deep-stone paper for the final picture. This helped considerably in establishing the middle tone, and can be seen in the buildings behind the trees, to the right. As you will by now be aware, the choice of the paper's tone is fairly important in pastel work. In this case, it enabled me to take a more direct approach with the pastel.

The finished painting of *Street nocturne*. 26 × 33 cm (10 × 13 in)

I began with a light tint of blue-grey for the sky area, rubbing this into the paper to give a smooth, soft tone. Against this, with a dark grey tint, I firmly drew in the roofs and chimneys of the buildings to the left, combining the tint in places with a dark purple-grey which I dragged down lightly for the lower walls, allowing the paper to show through. I changed to a dark brown for the deep tones of the buildings to the right behind the trees. I then applied a mid-grey for the softer tints of the distant buildings at the far end of the street.

I was now better able to deal with the light areas, first of all by using a cadmium red dragged on its side, making use of the texture of the paper to suggest rough walls. I pressed more firmly into the paper with yellow ochre and lemon yellow for the stronger highlights, together with a touch or two of cadmium red.

Next, I dealt with the lights across the foreground, some of which were of the same tones as the light walls and windows. I used light olive green on either side, merging into a darker shade of the same colour and red-grey

Balnakeil beach, daylight. 25 × 32 cm
(10 × 12½ in)

for the shadowed roadway in the centre. This left the dark trees, railings and figures to be dealt with in the foreground. I drew the bare trees in firmly with dark sepia, using the edge of the pastel. Black Conté crayon supplied the finer branches and the railings, and indicated the figures and a vehicle on the street.

The feeling that I strove to convey here was that of light and shade, with a sense of mystery in the shadows and along the street. In certain areas, such as in the sky and dark passages, I rubbed the pastel into the grain of the paper, while in the lighter parts I applied the pastel with a direct touch, which showed more of the grain and suggested texture on brickwork and other features. It was essential to keep the treatment of the buildings as direct and simple as possible, particularly in the shadows, in order to concentrate the main interest on the areas of light.

I made the study shown in *Balnakeil beach, daylight* in a remote part of Sutherland in north-west Scotland. This beach has always appealed to me, with its lovely stretch of sands which at low tide reflect the distant mountains fronted by lonely farm buildings. These buildings provide a feeling of scale and a focal point, especially in the evening when the lights from the farm reflect in the wet sands. I selected a soft grey

Balnakeil beach, twilight. 25 × 35 cm
(10 × 14 in)

pastel paper and drew in the main
shapes with a biro. I found this
useful for defining the outlines of
the buildings and mountains in
contrast to the soft reflections in
the wet sands, which were

obtained by rubbing in the pastel
to some extent. As the main theme
of this study was the wet sands,
I was careful not to allow the
distant mountains and buildings to
intrude, by keeping their shapes
and tones soft and distant.

For *Balnakeil beach, twilight* I
cast my mind back to the pleasant
experience of walking along the
beach as daylight merged into dusk
and the lights from the distant
farm buildings reflected in the wet
sands left by the receding tide.
I remembered the background
mountains softened by rising mists,
with the buildings and rocky

shoreline dark against them. I
chose a dark-toned paper for my
work in the studio, and, just as the
light grey paper had been helpful
in my daylight study, this helped
me to achieve the effect that I
wanted.

I began by using tones of light
blue-grey to indicate the distant
mountains. I followed this with a
paler grey, blending into light
burnt sienna for the luminous area
in the sky, with darker greys for
the clouds above. These provided
useful tones which, by contrast,
gave greater luminosity to the
light areas.

The tones of the lower slopes of the mountains behind the buildings were added next, with their edges blending into the mountains above. I then considered the dark buildings, together with the headlands in shadow to the left and right. I chose dark sepia for these passages, with black Conté crayon which gave a useful contrast with its dark tone. The buildings also made a strong contrast against the lights, and, together with their reflections, provided a focal point at a good place in the composition.

This, then, was my memory study, during which I had to create and maintain the softness and mystery of atmosphere appropriate to the effect of twilight. I have memories of high summer spent in these northern lands, when darkness did not descend further than twilight, and of long, dark winter nights illuminated and made dramatic by the Northern Lights (*Aurora Borealis*). These make an impressive sight when seen behind dark mountain peaks, a subject which I have not yet dared to attempt to paint.

Borth sands, daylight is, in many ways, similar to the *Balnakeil beach* paintings, both in the daylight study and its translation to the nocturne (shown overleaf). This led me to approach it in more or less the same way. I sketched this quick impression on the beach at Borth when the tide was out, leaving the sands wet and reflecting the figures and distant buildings. I worked rapidly to capture the effect before the return of the tide, on a piece of light grey sugar paper suitable for the rather high tonal key of the subject.

Borth sands, daylight. 24 × 38 cm (9½ × 15 in)

Borth sands, evening light. 25 × 35 cm
(10 × 14 in)

For *Borth sands, evening light* I
used a dark brown Canson paper.
I set a higher horizon in this
picture, to allow me to make
greater use of the reflections from
the light area of sky and the
buildings in artificial light (the
latter being enhanced by the dark
tones of the headland behind).
I used the broken posts of the
breakwater, together with their
reflections, to provide a little
interest and to create a tonal
contrast in the left foreground area
at the water's edge, which helped
to balance the dark tones of the
houses on the right. The distant
figures above the breakwater give a
feeling of life and a sense of scale
to the finished picture.

When I found the subject for *Burning the stubble*, I had been spending the day sketching up on the open Cotswolds, and was not very pleased with what I had produced. I was thinking of packing up when I happened to look round and see small fires being lit in the next field where corn had been cut and harvested, leaving stubble. Before long the separate fires began to unite and spread over the field, developing into quite an advancing army of flame. Against the fading light, this started to take on a definite dramatic effect, especially as the sky was darkening, producing a

subject much more lively and interesting than my rather pedestrian efforts of the day.

Some of the distant trees assumed a deep, cool grey tone behind the glowing flames and contrasted with them, as did other larger and darker trees closer to my position. I quickly established the strong darks and the lights against the deepening sky. Figures formed dark, silhouetted shapes against the flames as they worked to control the burning, and I drew these in as they appeared to provide human interest and a sense of scale. The trees and figures cast shadows across the foreground,

and reflected light illuminated the smoke drifting up against the sky. I used light cadmium reds and yellows for the flames, against the backdrop of distant blue- and purple-greys, with dark purple and autumn browns for the nearer trees.

Burning the stubble. 24 × 38 cm (9½ × 15 in)

119

Night fishing, Pembrokeshire.
25 × 35 cm (10 × 14 in)

When I painted *Night fishing, Pembrokeshire*, the light was fading from the evening sky and reflecting in the wet sands, and mists were softening the contours of the headlands. Groups of fishermen began to assemble with their gear, including lamps which created points of light.

I worked quickly to produce this fine subject on a deep-stone Ingres paper: this provided a helpful basic tone. The soft tones of the sky were reflected in the wet sands to the left of the foreground, contrasting with the dark rocks, and the darker browns of the cliffs to the right were also reflected. Using a black Conté crayon, I drew in the fishermen and their reflections firmly, and added the lamps and their reflections with light cadmium yellow. Bright touches of cadmium red gave me the lit-up figures with their reflections.

15

WORKING INDOORS

I am aware that many people find it difficult, or perhaps impossible, to work out of doors and would like to help them to find subject matter in their homes. I have mentioned elsewhere the possibility of painting views from windows when snow makes outside work difficult, but working from a window gives opportunities at any time. Room interiors – even a corner of a room or an item of furniture – can provide possibilities; remember what Van Gogh made of his bed and a simple chair. Study too, the interiors painted by the fine seventeenth-century artist Jan Vermeer.

The pink geranium presented an attractive focal point of colour, echoed in the curtain, in *Dining-room window*, which I painted on warm grey Canson paper. I needed to keep the shapes seen through the window simple, in order not to compete for interest with the items on the window-sill, which, along with the geranium, was lit by quite a strong light from outside. The dark, shadowed area of the wall beneath gave a strong contrast and firm basis to the composition. I drew everything in with a fine-pointed fibre-tipped pen, allowing the grey paper to show through in several places to create a tonal harmony.

Dining-room window. 29 × 30 cm (11½ × 12 in)

In *Through the kitchen window* the clematis climbing up the wall outside made a lovely focal point of light and colour in the sunlight. The pale Prussian blue sky, fading into the darker green-grey tones of the garden below, made a fine background contrast, which I kept simple, as in the dining-room picture. Once again, I drew in with a fine-pointed fibre-tipped pen on warm grey Canson paper. Dark sepia in the shadowed background tones of the clematis gave a strong contrast to the light flowers and the sunlit wall outside, all of which were reflected in the smooth tiles of the window-sill.

As in the previous two indoor studies, I found warm grey Canson paper a helpful support for *Still life, bottles etc.* (opposite), and once again I drew in with a fibre-tipped pen. I rubbed in the dark olive and grey-green tones of the bottles firmly to produce the smooth, polished effect of glass. These darks were in strong contrast to the clear wine glass, the orange and the warmer tones behind. The light from the window above illuminated the cloth, casting colourful shadows of the group across its surface.

(Left)
Through the kitchen window.
45 × 35 cm (17½ × 14 in)

(Opposite)
Still life, bottles, etc. 50 × 35 cm (19½ × 14 in)

16

STORAGE AND PRESENTATION

Protecting pastels from rubbing can often present problems, especially for someone who has not had any previous experience in dealing with them. Pictures can be sprayed with a fixative to prevent the pastel being rubbed off the surface of the paper, but this causes a darkening of the colours (most noticeable in the lighter tints) and may ruin the whole effect of the picture. For this reason I do not spray my work, but frame it up as soon as I can.

It may, however, be necessary to store pictures for a time until this is possible. On page 24, I described how I use my paper in such a way that the picture is protected by the folded section of the sheet. Covered up in this way, sketches can be put away in a folder until they are framed or needed for reference.

As for larger pictures, where it is not possible to fold over the same sheet, these can be protected by placing them between sheets of tissue or tracing-paper and holding them in position with paperclips or small pieces of masking tape to prevent lateral movement. As it is only movement over the surface of the work that causes damage, the pictures will withstand pressure from above while being stored. Storage in a drawer or cupboard with some kind of reference is, I find, the most convenient way of enabling one to find reference sketches as required.

Storm at sea. 41 × 51 cm (16 × 20 in)

MOUNTING AND FRAMING

Having chosen appropriate colours, I like to cut my own mounts on a machine which will take large sizes of mounting card: 81 × 112 cm (32 × 44 in) and 71 × 90 cm (28 × 35½ in). For the painting *Storm at sea* (opposite) I chose mount tones which repeated colours used in the picture. I used two thicknesses of mount, to which I added a strip of card about an inch wide, glued all round the back so that it could not be seen from the front. There were, therefore, three thicknesses of card between painting surface and glass, which would prevent any transference of pastel on to the glass.

I cut the window of the inner mount slightly smaller, in order to reveal 1·25 cm (½ in) of its lighter colour all round. The combined width of the two mounts was 6·25 cm (2½ in) at the top and sides, with 7·5 cm (3 in) at the base. The frame was 5 cm (2 in) in width and a light grey in colour (chosen to relate to the tones of the mounts and picture), with a gilt strip on its outer edge. I like to frame my work in sympathy with the general feeling of the picture, usually avoiding extremes of tone in both mount and frame.

For my paintings of *Nolton Haven* and *Breconshire landscape* I chose similar stone- and grey-coloured mounts, again with inner mounts of a lighter complementary tone. As with the first picture,

Nolton Haven. 41 × 51 cm (16 × 20 in)

these mounts repeated colours used in each painting to create a unified and well-balanced effect.

Breconshire landscape. 41 × 51 cm (16 × 20 in)

CONCLUSION

From the storm-lashed Sutherland coast to the quiet lanes of the Cotswolds, you, the reader, have travelled with me. We have known bleak winter snow and summer heat, heard the tumultuous roar of Niagara and walked beside a Scottish loch in the calm of twilight. We share a beautiful world, and for my part I try to respond to it in the way I know best, in terms of paint, to the approval or otherwise of the critics.

If I am able to convey to others some of my own feelings before nature, that makes it even more worthwhile. I admire the ways in which others have responded to the beauty of our landscape – be they painters, poets or musicians – and am uplifted by the open-air feeling of Housman, the majestic splendour of Beethoven, the graceful elegance of Mozart and the noble sadness of Elgar.

I hope that our experiences in these pages have given you pleasure, and that you have been helped and encouraged to persevere in your endeavours to respond to your own tastes and convictions.

Wildflowers. 43 × 30 cm (17 × 12 in)

AUBREY R. PHILLIPS
81.